DATE DUE

#47-0108 Peel Off Pressure Sensitive

Managing Technological Change

Managing Technological Change

Strategies for College and University Leaders

A. W. (Tony) Bates

Jossey-Bass Publishers • San Francisco

Jossey-Bass books and products are available through most bookstores. To contact Jossey-Bass directly, call (888) 378–2537, fax to (800) 605–2665, or visit our website at www.josseybass.com.

Substantial discounts on bulk quantities of Jossey-Bass books are available to corporations, professional associations, and other organizations. For details and discount information, contact the special sales department at Jossey-Bass.

TCF Manufactured in the United States of America on Lyons Falls Turin Book. This paper is acid-free and 100 percent totally chlorine-free.

Library of Congress Cataloging-in-Publication Data

Bates, Tony.
    Managing technological change : strategies for college and university leaders / A. W. (Tony) Bates. — 1st ed.
        p.   cm. — (The Jossey-Bass higher and adult education series)
    Includes bibliographical references (p.   ) and index.
    ISBN 0-7879-4681-8
        1. Education, Higher—Data processing.   2. Educational technology.
3. Education, Higher—Computer-assisted instruction.   4. Distance education.   5. Education, Higher—Effect of technological innovations on.
I. Title.   II. Series.
LB2395.7.B375   1999
378'.00285—dc21
                                                                99-44483

FIRST EDITION
HB Printing 10 9 8 7 6 5 4 3 2

The Jossey-Bass
Higher and Adult Education Series

Contents

List of Tables and Figures

Preface

If universities and colleges are successfully to adopt the use of technologies for teaching and learning, much more than minor adjustments in current practice will be required. Indeed, the effective use of technology requires a revolution in thinking about teaching and learning. Part of that revolution necessitates restructuring universities and colleges—that is, changing the way higher education institutions are planned, managed, and organized.

If we assume that the intelligent application of technology can improve learning, then what do we have to do to reorganize, restructure, or reengineer the university or college to ensure that its application of new technologies to teaching is also cost-effective? I try to answer that question in this book by

- Briefly exploring the context that is driving universities and colleges to adopt new technologies for teaching
- Suggesting a number of planning, management, and organizational strategies for universities and colleges to facilitate the effective use of new technologies for teaching
- Exploring the possible implications for universities and colleges of such restructuring

A subtext of this book is that academic staff need to control or "tame" the virtual campus by ensuring that technology is used as a tool or as a means to further academic ends. This control will not be achieved, however, without aggressive intervention on the part of academic leaders and faculty members.

One barrier to more effective use of technology for teaching is undoubtedly lack of technical skills. Students often have more advanced computer skills than their professors. However, this book suggests that although an element of technical training for professors may be valuable, lack of technical skill is not the main problem.

More frequently lacking are appropriate policies for the use of new technologies for teaching and sufficient technical support for instructors.

Another barrier to the more extensive use of technology is fear of its possible negative aspects on academic life. Some concerns about the impact of new technologies on teaching and learning are legitimate, and I do attempt to address some of these concerns in the book. Nevertheless, technology can be a valuable academic asset if used wisely, but this means understanding both the educational potential and limitations of technology for teaching, and above all, learning how to manage and control it.

Intended Audience

This book is aimed at key decision makers in the academic communities of universities and colleges, including heads of departments, deans, vice presidents, and presidents. It is also aimed at faculty members concerned with teaching and learning policies and practices, as well as elected representatives in faculty associations and unions. This is not a book aimed primarily at technology specialists, although I hope that many will read this so that they too will understand the academic and educational requirements and implications of the new technologies. It is likely to be of particular interest to professionals in educational technology support areas, such as faculty development officers, directors of educational technology support units, and managers of campus information technology services.

Contents

The book starts with an Executive Summary of the main conclusions and recommendations. The next chapter, Chapter One, looks at the forces leading to change in higher education institutions, and in particular the impact of new technologies on these changes, and discusses some of the educational benefits and limitations of the technologies. I feel it is important that the potential of technology for teaching and learning be fully understood, because planning and management decisions should be strongly influenced by an understanding of the educational strengths and weaknesses. The chapter also provides some case studies illustrating the dramatic way in which technology can transform teaching and learning in universities and colleges.

Chapters Two to Nine, which form the heart of the book, describe a wide range of strategies for planning and managing new technologies for teaching and learning. Chapter Ten discusses the implications of the recommended strategies for higher education institutions and raises questions about the capacity and desirability of existing institutions moving so dramatically into new forms of organization.

Acknowledgments

No book is ever the work of just one person. I have drawn more than most authors on the ideas and experiences of many people and organizations. I am privileged to work in an area where people are generous with their time, their ideas, and their work.

First, I would like to acknowledge the help and encouragement of my colleagues at the University of British Columbia (UBC). Many of the strategies described in this book originated from the process of managing the university's innovation fund in 1994–95 and 1995–96. Bernie Sheehan, currently president of the Technical University of British Columbia, then Barry McBride, now academic vice president at UBC, chaired the relevant committees that developed strategies and processes for managing the application of technology to teaching and learning. The members of these committees are too numerous to mention individually, but they were the source of many ideas that contributed to policy development. I would also like to acknowledge the major contribution of Dan Birch, vice president, academic, and provost at the time. He not only initiated and coordinated the early efforts at UBC to put in place policies and processes for encouraging the use of technology but also gave me tremendous support and encouragement as a new member of UBC's staff working in this area. I have also received wise advice and valuable information from Ted Dodds, UBC's associate vice president for information technology services. Last, I would like to acknowledge the special support I have received from Walter Uegama, associate vice president, continuing studies, to whom I report.

This book draws on experience from personal visits to over twenty different higher education institutions in the United States, Canada, Mexico, and Australia. It also draws on studies, in which I participated, of three state higher education systems in the United States and two provinces of Canada.

Some of the institutions I visited and from which experience has been drawn for this book are as follows: University of Maine at Orono; University of Southern Maine, Portland; University of Maine at Augusta; Educational Network of Maine; Indiana University, Bloomington; Ball State University, Muncie; Indiana State University, Terre Haute; Ivy Tech University, Indianapolis; IHETS and Access Indiana, Indianapolis; Virginia Tech, Blacksburg; Florida State University, Tallahassee; Florida Gulf Coast University, Fort Myers; Center for Distributed Learning, California State University, Rohnert Park; State Higher Education Executive Officers Association, Denver; American Productivity & Quality Center, Houston; McGill University, Montreal; University of Calgary, Alberta; University of Alberta, Edmonton; Collège Boréal, Sudbury, Ontario; Murdoch University, Perth, Australia; Edith Cowan University, Perth, Australia; Deakin University, Geelong, Victoria, Australia; University of Melbourne, Victoria; University of Queensland, Brisbane, Australia; Queensland University of Technology, Brisbane, Australia; Monterrey Institute of Technology, Monterrey, Mexico; University of Nuevo Leon, Monterrey; and University of Guadalajara, Mexico.

It should be pointed out that I usually visited these institutions as a consultant or by invitation to discuss with management the use of technology for teaching, not to collect material for this book. However, out of the presentations, questions, and discussions, inevitably a number of ideas and strategies were born.

Everywhere I went, I found great interest in the topic of managing academic technologies and an openness to share experience and learn from others. This is perhaps the most important finding of my study, and it offers great hope for the future of universities and colleges in North America and Australia. I would like to mention in particular the University of Calgary, Virginia Tech, and Collège Boréal, which all provided exceptionally valuable information.

Much of this book was developed in the process of offering an on-line graduate course on planning and managing technology-based distributed learning. In this endeavor I was helped greatly by Mark Bullen and Diane Janes, my colleagues in UBC's distance education and technology unit. The on-line contributions of many of the students in this course were also a valuable source of ideas on planning and management. Any academic rigor detected in this book is due mainly to Dan Pratt, Roger Boshier, Tom Sork, and Hans Schuetze, from UBC's department of educational studies, who provided academic approval for the course and gave invaluable advice on content and method. I would be delighted if readers joined other professionals in challenging the ideas and concepts in the book by enrolling in this course (EDST 533; http://itesm. cstudies.ubc.ca/info).

I am also indebted to Jim Mingle and Rhonda Epper from the State Higher Education Executive Officers Association and to Marisa Brown and her team at the American Productivity & Quality Center (APQC). Jim Mingle has been a superb colleague, opening many doors for me, and contributing many ideas on the planning and management of technology in universities and state higher education systems. Rhonda Epper was the main writer and author of the APQC study on faculty instructional development in the use of technology for teaching and again has been extremely generous in sharing her ideas and knowledge. The APQC study enabled me to visit several institutions at which I was able to obtain information that has been invaluable for this book. I am most grateful to APQC and the various institutions for permission to use this material. (More information on APQC and its activities in the use of technology in education can be found at its Web site: http://www.apqc.org.) I would also like to thank Diana Oblinger, academic programs and strategy executive, IBM, for advice and information on developments on the use of technology in higher education in North America.

With all the help I have had, there is no excuse for getting things wrong. However, I must accept responsibility for the views and information contained in this book. Much to my surprise, many of my colleagues do not always agree with me, and I should make it plain that this book reflects my opinions, not necessarily those of my colleagues or the institutions that contributed to this book.

September 1999   A. W. (TONY) BATES
Vancouver, British Columbia, Canada

The Author

A. W. (TONY) BATES is responsible for developing distance education programs and flexible delivery of credit and noncredit programs at the University of British Columbia (UBC), in conjunction with faculty and program directors. He is project leader for a research study on cost-benefit analysis of on-line teaching for the Canadian National Center of Excellence in Telelearning. He is also project leader for a study of the impact of technology on adult learners for the Canadian Federal Office of Learning Technologies.

Before moving to UBC, he was executive director of research, strategic planning, and information technology at the Open Learning Agency (OLA) of British Columbia, where he worked from 1990 to 1995. Prior to that, he was professor of educational media research at the British Open University, where he worked for 20 years and was one of the founding members of staff.

Bates has worked as a consultant in over thirty countries and for several U.S. state higher education commissions on educational technology planning. His research groups at the British Open University, OLA, and UBC have published over 350 papers in the area of distance education and the use of technology for teaching.

Bates is the author of five books, including *Technology, Open Learning, and Distance Education* (1995), which won a National Universities Continuing Education Association award for the best book on distance education in 1995. Also, in 1995 he was awarded the degree of Doctor Honoris Causa by the Open University of Portugal for his research in distance education. Bates received his Ph.D. degree in Educational Administration from the University of London, England, in 1972.

Executive Summary

Decision makers like to "cut to the chase." I have therefore pulled together the book's main conclusions and recommendations in this Executive Summary.

 • *New technologies such as the World Wide Web and multimedia have the potential to widen access to new learners, increase flexibility for "traditional" students, and improve the quality of teaching by achieving higher levels of learning, such as analysis, synthesis, problem solving, and decision making.* These new technologies can also be used to develop learners' skills in seeking, analyzing, and interpreting information relevant to their subject domain (Chapter One).

 • *New technologies are unlikely to lead to a reduction in spending by higher education institutions, at least in the short term, because of the high and recurrent cost of investment.* Still, under the right circumstances new technologies can lead to improved cost-effectiveness by enabling new target groups to be reached and higher-quality learning outcomes to be gained at a lower marginal cost per student than through conventional classroom methods. To achieve these gains in cost-effectiveness, though, teaching and learning need to be substantially reorganized (Chapters One and Six).

 • *History suggests that the introduction of new technology is usually accompanied by major changes in the organization of work.* New technologies are associated with postindustrial forms of organization based on highly skilled and flexible workers with a good degree of autonomy organized into relatively small and flexible operational units. In contrast, universities and colleges have been characterized by a mixture of agrarian and industrial forms of organization, with hierarchical, bureaucratic, and relatively inflexible organizational structures and procedures, although the autonomy of tenured faculty maintains an element of flexibility, and in some respects, chaos. If new technology is usually accompanied by major changes in the organization of work, then the introduction of new technologies for teaching will require a major shift toward postindustrial forms of organization for universities and colleges (Chapters Two and Seven).

- *The use of technology needs to be embedded within a wider strategy for teaching and learning.* Teaching departments need to develop concrete, innovative, future-oriented plans for teaching that take account not only of changes in technology but also other changes in society that should influence their work. These departmental teaching plans should influence, be guided by, and be integrated into broader institutional plans. Two critical strategies for doing this are "visioning" exercises and a flexible and continuous strategic planning process. Institutional leadership of a high quality will be required to manage these processes (Chapter Two).

- *The increased ease of use of new technologies has led to the development of "Lone Ranger" approaches to technology-based teaching.* The Lone Ranger is an individual faculty member working independently except for the assistance of a graduate student. The Lone Ranger approach is a useful means by which to get faculty members started in using new technologies, but it is a costly and inefficient method of teaching with new technologies. For high-quality, cost-effective results, a project management approach is recommended, based on funding tied to clearly articulated project objectives, teamwork, and defined budgets and production schedules (Chapter Three).

- *Appropriate technology infrastructure is an essential requirement for technology-based teaching.* This means adequate technology support staff for faculty members as well as networks, hardware, and software. Furthermore, the technology infrastructure has to serve both administrative and academic needs. Nevertheless, it is essential that investment in technology infrastructure be influenced and guided by academic as well as administrative priorities. This in turn requires the development of academic plans and priorities for teaching with technology, and planning mechanisms that ensure that both academic and administrative requirements are fully considered. It is important to strike a balance in investment between infrastructure and educational applications of technology (Chapter Four).

• *There is a tension between the need for students to have access to technology, and issues of equity and universal access to higher education.* However, in the long run, it will become economically unsustainable for a university or college to provide all the facilities on campus needed for student access to computers. It many cases it will be better to require students to provide their own computers and to focus financial and other help on those who most need it. Every department and institution will need to have a clearly articulated and well-communicated policy regarding student computer requirements. There must be clearly identified "value-added" learning benefits to justify the requirement for students to have a computer, and this needs to be built into the curriculum (Chapter Four).

• *Faculty members need much more support and encouragement than has been provided to date for their use of technology for teaching and learning.* It is now essential to place greater emphasis on overall teaching ability for appointment, tenure, and promotion, even in research universities, and the successful use of technology should be one criterion to be considered in assessing teaching performance. Teaching with technology requires a high skill level, and this necessitates training not just in technical matters but also in educational practice. Training needs to be embedded in the course development process, and the project management model can assist this. In addition to training, faculty members need greater levels of technical and educational support staff than has been provided to date (Chapter Five).

• *All faculty members must understand and comply with copyright law.* Institutions need to negotiate with staff clearly defined agreements regarding ownership of materials developed in the course of teaching. The project management model provides a structure for doing this. Institutions need specialists to advise on copyright and intellectual property and to ensure that there is compliance both with the law and with institutional policies (Chapter Five).

• *It is essential that institutions understand the costs of using new technologies.* A method for costing Web-based teaching, including the pricing of fully cost-recoverable courses, is described. Although cost analysis is still heavily influenced by the assumptions made about what costs to include or exclude, it is possible to assess the costs of technology-based teaching reasonably accurately. One significant obstacle to its accurate costing is the lack of activity-based accounting procedures in many higher education institutions, in addition to the lack of detailed costing methods for attributing costs to conventional teaching (Chapter Six).

•   *Funding is probably the biggest lever for change.* Various strategies for funding technology-based teaching and learning are examined, including external grants, student technology fees, and reallocation. Reallocation is the ultimate test of an institution's commitment to teaching with technology. It is difficult to see how an institution can make doing so a primary strategy without some very difficult decisions about reallocation of base operating funds. Eventually, funding decisions on technology-based teaching need to be pushed down to the departmental level, with central funding for institutionwide infrastructure and specialized technical and educational support. In the short term, though, centralized funding may be necessary to encourage project management approaches and the commitment to teaching with technology (Chapter Seven).

•   *Partnerships and collaboration are strategies for sharing the costs and leveraging the benefits of technology-based teaching.* Several models of partnership and collaboration are described and assessed, and the requirements for successful partnerships are identified. Successful partnerships require time and financial investment and should be strategic; the potential benefits need to be clearly defined and understood by all parties. In the end, however, successful partnerships depend on individual faculty members being able to work collaboratively with their counterparts in the other organizations (Chapter Seven).

•   *An organizational structure encompassing a mix of centralized and decentralized strategies is recommended to support teaching with technology.* The mix will depend to some extent on the size of the organization. Every faculty and large department will need some technical and educational support located in the department or faculty. However, most institutions will also need centralized services with specialist technical equipment and staff with specialist skills who can work with individual faculties and departments. It is recommended that at least 5 percent of the base teaching budget be devoted to technical and educational support for teaching with technology, and a model for organizing such support is described (Chapter Eight).

•   *As the institution starts to use technology for teaching outside its local area, new administrative and academic procedures will be necessary in the areas of admissions, finance, and academic policy.* Eventually, distributed technologies will result in the creation of relatively small, autonomous, integrated, and self-contained teaching and administrative units in a larger institution. Last, management structures need to be put in place at a senior level to ensure that academic priorities and strategies for the use of technology are integrated with administrative requirements (Chapter Eight).

•   *Given the emerging context of technology-based teaching, especially for traditional campus-based universities and colleges, research and evaluation will be essential.* Results from recent cost-benefit research are summarized. The following areas of technology-based teaching require further study: student access issues, cost-benefit analysis (especially indirect costs and benefits), the relationship between different technology applications and different learning outcomes, the balance of face-to-face and technology-based teaching and the impact on different kinds of learners, on-line tutoring strategies, educational and technical design of learning materials, appropriate teaching software, and appropriate management and organizational structures for supporting technology-based learning (Chapter Nine).

•   *The implementation of these strategies will require fundamental change in the way our higher education institutions are organized and managed.* They will affect the nature of the work of faculty members, and above all will affect the relationship between teachers and learners. As technology increasingly permeates and changes the teaching environment, it will become increasingly important to define very clearly the purpose and unique features of face-to-face teaching and the role of the campus and to identify those learners for whom these features have the most relevance (Chapter Ten).

•   *Finally, the changes proposed in this book may be too rich, too drastic, or too threatening to the core values of many institutions.* I do not argue that institutions should necessarily adopt technology extensively for teaching. However, if they make the decision to do so, then the strategies proposed in this book will be necessary to justify the high cost of investment that will follow from such a decision (Chapter Ten).

This Executive Summary neither captures the details of how to implement the various recommended strategies nor, more important, discusses the relative advantages and disadvantages of each. It also does not provide the context from which these conclusions and recommendations are drawn. Because context is critical for determining policy and strategies in this area, I hope this Executive Summary will provide sufficient stimulus for you to read the rest of the book.

Chapter One

Confronting the Technology Challenge in Universities and Colleges

Carol Twigg (quoted in Marchese, 1998) dramatically but accurately illustrated the unprecedented challenge to universities and colleges resulting from the impact of new technology: "What was once a competitive advantage [for universities and colleges]—the physical concentration of intellectual resources on a residential campus—is no longer a critical differentiator. Newer information age models, which are distributed and ultimately network-based, eliminate many of the advantages of vertical integration, making it easy for many different types of competitors to enter the marketplace rapidly."

Daryl Le Grew, the former academic vice president of Deakin University, Australia, has pointed out that many postsecondary institutions "are moving to reconstruct their infrastructure, redesign policy, and realign external relationships to gain comparative advantage in the information superhighway environment" (Le Grew, 1995). He argues that there is a transformation—a "paradigm shift"—taking place in postsecondary education, characterized by the following trends:

From	*To*
Industrial society	Information society
Technology peripheral	Multimedia central
Once-only education	Lifelong learning

Fixed curriculum	Flexible, open curriculum
Institutional focus	Learner focus
Self-contained organization	Partnerships
Local focus	Global networking

In particular, Le Grew argues that the new technological environment "opens access to study across sectoral, disciplinary, and cultural boundaries," and that this "will quickly erode traditional ideas of the course of study." Le Grew is not alone in his predictions. Recent publications by Dolence and Norris (1995), Mason (1998), Rowley, Lujan, and Dolence (1998), Marchese (1998), and Katz and Associates (1999) all present similar conclusions.

Why the Need for Change?

There are many interrelated reasons for this pressure on higher education institutions to change. I have chosen three that are of particular significance as the themes of this book:

- The need to do more with less
- The changing learning needs of society
- The impact of new technologies on teaching and learning

Doing More with Less

Since the late 1960s, the number of students in postsecondary public education around the world has steadily expanded. Many more postsecondary institutions have been created over the last ten years.

In general, this expansion has not been accompanied by a pro rata increase in funding. In the United States, the cost of higher education has steadily increased year by year. It has increased not merely as a gross amount but also in average cost per student and cost of tuition paid by students or their parents. For instance, tuition fees at public higher education institutions in the United States have nearly doubled in the last twenty years after adjustment for inflation (Institute for Higher Education Policy, 1999).

There are several reasons for this situation. Following the rapid expansion of higher education in the 1960s, the professoriate has been steadily aging, leading to salary creep. As governments try to eliminate public debt and deficits, there has been increasing fiscal restraint. Last, there has been growing public disenchantment with higher education institutions, whose preoccupations and methods of operation often seem to the public to be increasingly divorced from the needs and expectations of the wider society. As one British vice chancellor put it, "Universities now operate in a low-trust environment." Consequently, in the United States, contributions from state and federal government to public higher education institutions have dropped from 59 percent in 1980–81 to 47 percent in 1994–95 (Institute for Higher Education Policy, 1999).

In Canada, most provincial governments have required universities and colleges to take on more students while maintaining or even reducing levels of funding. In Australia and some parts of Canada (Ontario and Alberta), some universities have had their operating grants from government reduced by up to 25 percent over a two- or three-year period.

The impact on the classroom has been severe. The increase in students has been handled by increases in class size, which inevitably means less individual interaction with senior tenured faculty and less individual attention for students. Young teaching assistants have been hired, often only a few years ahead in their studies of those they are teaching. Sometimes these teaching assistants are international graduate students whose English is poor. Teaching assistants are often assigned mainly to teach large undergraduate classes so that more senior research professors can teach smaller classes of higher-level undergraduate or graduate students. But with the increase in associate degree programs and transfers from two-year colleges, even third- and fourth-level classes have grown to a large size in many institutions.

Finally, many faculty members—whose own experience was formed as students attending university when doing so was reserved for a relatively small elite—have never come to terms with the implications of "mass" higher education. They view with genuine distress the lack of interaction and communication that results from large class size and the impact on their research time of increasingly demanding administrative and teaching duties.

Many faculty members now recognize that these unpleasant circumstances are unlikely to go away. Unless significant changes are made, universities and colleges will find themselves in a downward spiral, as costs and class sizes continue to rise and the students, the public, and the politicians become increasingly reluctant to support what rightly or wrongly are seen as increasingly self-serving and inefficient institutions.

Changing Learning Needs

While coping with a deteriorating instructor-student ratio, universities and colleges are being asked to meet new needs. One is the need for a much more highly skilled workforce to enable a nation to remain economically competitive and to sustain a prosperous society based on high wages (Porter, 1991).

The sources of employment have rapidly changed because of increased automation and the growth of new industries and services, such as telecommunications, information technology, and financial services. Although traditional manufacturing industries and government services are shedding labor, most new jobs are being created in private sector service industries and in companies employing fewer than twenty people. Where jobs are being created in the larger manufacturing industries, they often require highly skilled specialists, each new employee often replacing many existing lesser-skilled staff.

Many of the new jobs are on a part-time or contract basis—with at least two-thirds of the new jobs going to women—and a majority of new jobs are relatively low paid (Kunin, 1988). Nevertheless, nearly half the new jobs created require graduates or people with the equivalent of seventeen years of full-time education (Canadian Labour Market Productivity Center, 1989).

Thus the traditional picture of work as a lifetime commitment to a particular trade or institution with a secure pension at the end applies to an increasingly smaller proportion of the population. In particular, secure middle management jobs of a general kind, requiring little or no professional or technical expertise, are disappearing rapidly. A very small proportion of the young men and women leaving school will find employment in the traditional resource-based or manufacturing industries as unskilled or semi-skilled workers. Most of those already unemployed, and a good proportion of those already working in large companies or in manufacturing or resource-based industries, will need to be retrained every few years.

The most significant development is that many of the new jobs being created require a much higher skill level than the jobs they are replacing, especially in management and manufacturing industries. People will retain existing jobs only if they are reeducated to higher standards; even for the majority of new jobs that are low paid and require generally low skill levels, training or retraining will be necessary, especially in basic skills, just in order to keep the job.

With respect to the new skills needed in the workforce, the Conference Board of Canada (1991) has defined them well:

- Good communication skills (reading, writing, speaking, listening)
- Ability to learn independently
- Social skills (ethics, positive attitude, responsibility)
- Teamwork skills
- Ability to adapt to changing circumstances
- Thinking skills (problem solving; critical, logical, numerical skills)
- Knowledge navigation (knowing where to get and how to process information)

Thus the education and training of the workforce is now a high priority for governments, and this education and training must be continued throughout a person's lifetime because of the continuing pressure to remain competitive. It has been argued that investment in education and training is now as essential for company survival in a knowledge-based economy as capital or plant investment (Reich, 1991).

It is hard to quantify the need for workforce education and training. However, if we assume that a person will need to retrain at least five times in a working lifetime and that such retraining requires the equivalent of three months of full-time learning (probably a gross underestimate), then the current capacity of the Canadian education and training market, public and private, probably needs to be at least doubled (Open Learning Agency, 1992).

The need for this increased capacity results from increased demand from two sources. The first is from young people continuing into postsecondary education. This demand will continue to increase slightly in most developed countries (between 2 percent and 5 percent per annum for another ten years at least) as more and more young people realize the importance of further education for their future prosperity. Many professors also feel that with the widening of access, the range of academic ability of freshmen students has widened. Professors are now teaching many students who would have not entered higher education in the past. Many campuses are witnessing a significant increase in students from minority populations and from different cultures. This challenges professors to deal with wide differences in prior learning, language and communication abilities, and cultural assumptions.

At the same time, universities and colleges are facing an important increase in demand from all those in the workforce who need to continue learning if they are to stay employed and if their employers are to remain economically competitive. This new market's requirements for learning are very different from those of the young people the higher education system has traditionally served.

Learning in the workplace will be initiated by individuals as part and parcel of their working and leisure lives. It will be informal (that is, not leading to any formal qualification), self-directed, and piecemeal (broken into small chunks of learning, some as small as a few minutes a day). It will be driven as much by short-term needs as by any conscious plan of study. Thus, it will not be determined by some master instructor but rather by the task at hand (Weimer, 1992).

To understand just how prevalent this kind of learning is already, just ask yourself how you have learned to use a computer. How much of it was the result of formal training with an instructor, and how much was picked up piecemeal by trial and error, with a poor manual, and with help from colleagues? This is not to say that the learning would not have been much more effective if it *had* been structured and directed all through by a skilled tutor, but what drives such learning is not the control of an instructor but the needs and the motivation of the learner.

Traditionally, large companies have provided training for their employees by establishing their own training centers and programs; small- and medium-size companies have relied more on outsourcing the training to private training companies or to public sector institutions. All of these methods, however, are labor-intensive, and any increase in such activities would lead to proportional increases in cost at a time when companies are under pressure to be more cost-competitive.

Furthermore, in the new economy, modern workers are much more mobile, moving from employer to employer or increasingly working for themselves. Therefore, they want "portable" qualifications, that is, qualifications that have some independent validity, either for their own satisfaction, if they are self-employed, or for their new employer.

Finally, many employers and members of the public are growing increasingly critical of the quality of education being provided through the public sector. There seems to be a mismatch between the skills taught and the requirements of the labor market (see, for example, the British Columbia Labor Force Development Board, 1995).

In some ways, this is an unfair criticism. Educational attainment of students in public schools has increased over the last twenty years; the problem is that the demands on the workforce have increased at an even faster rate (Drouin, 1990). For instance, production line workers need greater literacy skills today to deal with written instructions, manuals, and so forth. They now need more than just an arm and a leg to operate the production machinery; they need intellectual skills as well. Similarly, with greater emphasis on teamwork and worker involvement and motivation, the level of communication and social skills required from managers and supervisors has increased.

Although a great deal of attention is being paid to the gap between the skills of those entering the workplace and the needs of employers, less attention is being paid to the much wider gap between the skills of those already in the workforce and the demands of the workplace. For instance, the older the worker, the lower the functional literacy level in most developed countries.

Impact of New Technologies on Learning

Modern learning theory sees learning as an individual quest for meaning and relevance. Once learning moves beyond the recall of facts, principles, or correct procedures and into the area of creativity, problem solving, analysis, or evaluation (the very skills needed in the workplace in a knowledge-based economy, not to mention in life in general), learners need the opportunity to communicate with one another as well as with their teachers. This of course includes the opportunity to question, challenge, and discuss issues. Learning is as much a social as an individual activity.

This learning requirement should not cause distress or concern to instructors in the higher education system, particularly those in the liberal arts area. However, learners not only need the liberal arts skills but *also* need them integrated with specialized knowledge in areas such as business, information technology, science, or engineering. Furthermore, they need this knowledge delivered in different ways from the traditional campus-based classroom.

These changes in the workforce highlight the gap between the way educational services are currently provided and the needs of employers and working people. Working people are unable or cannot afford to give up jobs or move house to become full-time or even part-time campus-based students again. They are increasingly looking for more flexible and more responsive forms of education and training.

For instance, if someone is working in a small company, the nearest person with similar interests and expertise may be on the other side of the country, particularly when it comes to leading-edge technologies. That person may or may not be an instructor at a college or university. Those seeking professional expertise will look to new information technologies to find the expertise that they need.

Learners will increasingly interact through their desktop or portable workstations in a variety of ways, determined by the nature of the learning task and their preferred style of learning in the work situation. These preferred styles will vary considerably. Different people will have different preferred learning styles. Even the same person may have different preferred learning styles for different tasks.

The learning context will need to enable people to work alone, interacting with learning material (which may be available locally or remotely); work collaboratively (and in an equal relationship) with fellow workers at different remote sites; learn as an "apprentice" or "student" working with a more experienced worker, supervisor, or instructor; and work as an instructor, supervisor, or more experienced colleague for other, less experienced colleagues.

The same person may find herself in each of these roles in a single working day. Learners will also need to be able to work from home, from a work site, or while traveling. They will need to be able to access information (searching, downloading) from multiple sources in multiple formats; select, store, and reorder or re-create information; directly communicate with instructors, colleagues, and other learners; incorporate accessed or reworked material into work documents; share and manipulate information, documents, or projects with others; and access, combine, create, and transmit audio, video, text, and data as necessary. If we take this as a design requirement for teaching and learning, there is then a need to build systems that support this, both for formal and for informal learning.

Especially in research universities, many faculty members may question whether providing lifelong learning, especially for those in the workforce, is an appropriate mandate. They may consider this to be something that can best be done by the private training sector.

This is a strategic issue for publicly funded institutions. Publicly funded research helps create new knowledge. The public may feel that they have a right to access the new knowledge being created through public taxes. Indeed, more than any other higher education institution, the publicly funded research university may be seen as having a major obligation to support lifelong learning. It would be a high-risk strategy for a research university to decide that it will ignore the teaching and learning needs of this major and rapidly developing market.

Thus, although new technologies are being used predominantly to serve the more traditional, full-time, on-campus student, a massive market is now emerging for which these new technologies will have even more relevance for teaching and learning. The intelligent use of new technologies provides an opportunity for universities and colleges to address both markets in a more cost-effective way than through traditional methods of teaching and learning.

Different Rationales for Using Technology for Teaching in Higher Education

A number of factors are leading many postsecondary institutions to experiment with new information technologies for teaching. Here are six of the most frequent reasons given for using technology (although there are probably many more):

- To improve the quality of learning
- To provide students with the everyday information technology skills they will need in their work and life
- To widen access to education and training
- To respond to the "technological imperative"
- To reduce the costs of education
- To improve the cost-effectiveness of education

Different people in different positions tend to place different emphasis on each of these rationales.

Improving the Quality of Teaching

Certainly in large research universities, this has been the major driver behind the increased interest in using new technologies for teaching. Increased student-to-teacher ratios, increased teaching loads, use of inexperienced or predoctoral teaching assistants, and the lack of interaction and reduced contact between tenured faculty and students at an undergraduate level have led to growing dissatisfaction with the current classroom teaching environment. The use of technology is seen as one way of easing or alleviating some of these problems. We will discuss the perceived benefits in more detail in the following sections.

Providing Technology Skills for Work and Life

Another reason is the need to prepare students for a world where information technology is likely to be central to their work and everyday lives. It will become increasingly difficult to accept people as being fully educated if they do not know how to use the Internet to communicate with other professionals, if they do not know how to find Web sites that will provide relevant and reliable information in their field of study, or if they do not know how to develop their own multimedia reports for communicating their knowledge or research. Integrating these technologies into the teaching environment is an obvious way to help students develop such skills.

Widening Access and Increasing Flexibility

As a distance educator, this is one of my primary reasons for being interested in technology. My job is to help make available the expertise of on-campus faculty members to those who cannot access the campus. Enabling that expertise to be accessed by off-campus students requires the use of many different kinds of technology, from print to multimedia CD-ROMs, depending on the needs and the circumstances of the targeted learners.

However, there are pressures to make learning more flexible even for those students who *can* access the campus. There has been a rapid increase in the number of campus-based students who are working part-time as a result of escalating costs (fees, living expenses, travel) and fear that they will end their studies with huge personal debt. With the best will in the world, it is often difficult for such students to avoid having lecture timetables clash with job obligations; yet if denied the opportunity for part-time work, many of them would be denied the opportunity of higher education.

Also, the trend toward lifelong learning and the need for reeducation and training for people already in the workforce are leading to a changing student population, with many more older students, working and with families, returning to postsecondary education (or in some cases never leaving it). These students need greater flexibility in the provision of learning, to fit it around their already busy and demanding lives.

The rapid rate of change in the workplace is also requiring all graduates to continue to be lifelong learners. In many professions today it is essential to update knowledge and skills on a continual basis. However, the requirements of this target group are very different from those of full-time or even part-time students coming directly from high schools.

Because lifelong learners are already in the workforce, it is impractical for them to attend a campus on a regular and frequent basis. Furthermore, they often do not need full degree programs but rather short courses, certificates, or diplomas, or even "just-in-time" training in small modules. Also, this target group is often able and willing to afford the full cost of such programs, thus bringing a department much-needed revenue. The flexible delivery of courses and programs through new technologies has many advantages for this target group.

Responding to the Technological Imperative

One rationale that leads to great opposition to the use of technology for teaching in academic circles is the *technological imperative*, that is, we have to use technology because of a blind belief that it is good for us. If we don't agree to the use of technology, we will be considered out of date and may lose our credibility.

Those who challenge the technological imperative do so from a variety of positions. Some ask what technology is doing to our ways of thinking and understanding (for example, Postman, 1992). The answer usually is that it weakens our ability to think rationally or logically. Others go further and suggest that the pressure to use technology (in all walks of life, but particularly in education) is a conspiracy by multinational companies and big business to sell technology and to hook young people forever as technology consumers (see Noble, 1997, 1998). Others recognize the pressure to be fashionable and to have the latest toys and lever that attitude to win support for their technology-based teaching initiatives, but they still believe there are educational benefits in using technology for teaching.

Those like myself who believe that technology can play a valuable role in teaching and learning see arguments against the technological imperative as valid but insufficient to deny it. As Feenberg (1999) puts it: "The overselling of foolish ideas about technology should not be allowed to discredit the whole field of on-line education. We as faculty need to get beyond defensive contempt for this significant educational innovation and look at specific designs with legitimate pedagogical objectives in mind."

Reducing Costs

This is a rationale more likely to come from politicians, the business community, government officials, and senior managers than from faculty members or department heads. However, to assume that investment in technology will lead to reduced cost in higher education is to misunderstand the nature of the educational process in higher education and the relationship of technology to that process. Indeed, the introduction of technology is more likely to lead to *increased* rather than reduced costs, at least in the short term. There are several reasons for this.

First, there is a high cost of investment in technological infrastructure (networks, computers, technical support staff). Furthermore, technology is changing rapidly. The average life of a computer is often less than four years, and word-processing and specialized software for creating materials, such as PowerPoint, WebCT, or Director, are constantly being updated and improved.

There is also a high and continuing cost of staff development. A steep learning curve has to be climbed by faculty members before new technologies start to deliver the benefits they promise. Climbing that learning curve demands a heavy investment of time from all staff, a point that will be addressed in more detail later in this book. Even when faculty members become skilled in using technology, they need constantly to update and improve their skills as the technology changes.

Although technology can replace some aspects of teaching and can enhance or facilitate communication between teachers and students, and especially those who cannot access the campus, good quality teaching in higher education still needs high levels of teacher-student interaction if creative, critical, and analytical thinking and good communications skills are to be achieved. Higher education therefore is likely to remain "people-intensive." In a knowledge-based society, there is no point in merely reducing cost if it also leads to lower-quality graduates.

Improving the Cost-Effectiveness of Higher Education

Last, some look to technology to improve the cost-effectiveness of education. This is not the same as reducing costs. The argument is that for the same dollar expenditure learning effectiveness can be increased or that more students can be taught to the same standard for the same level of investment.

In fact, although technology is unlikely to reduce absolute costs, it can improve the cost-effectiveness of operations in higher education in several ways: by enabling institutions to reach out to more and different students; by reducing or eliminating those activities currently carried out by instructors that are better done by technology, thus freeing faculty members for more productive use of their time; and by improving the quality of learning, either by enabling new skills and learning outcomes to be achieved or by enabling students to achieve existing learning goals more easily or more quickly.

This book attempts to look at what is needed to achieve such goals.

Conflicting Rationales

It is worth noting that faculty members supporting one rationale for using technology for teaching may actually violently oppose another rationale. For instance, the same professor who is a startling innovator in the use of the technology for improving his teaching may violently oppose any suggestion that more students might be served by the institution through the use of his material. Other professors are fired up by the idea that all the world is waiting to access their ideas, their research, their wisdom through the World Wide Web—a passion to widen access to their expertise. This is not always accompanied, though, by a similar passion to improve the quality of their teaching, as can be witnessed by surfing their Web pages, which may be bereft of good educational design features.

It is important that teachers and institutional decision makers be clear about their reasons for using technology, because it will affect their choice and management of technology. For instance, if widening access and increasing enrollments are the main reasons, then more advanced and expensive technologies need to be avoided. If, however, high-quality teaching using expert systems is the goal, then the use of advanced multimedia technology might be justified.

Can the Virtual University Really Teach?

At this point we need to examine more closely the claim that teaching with technology can lead to an improved quality of learning.

The basic university or college teaching paradigm for most subjects has not changed a great deal in the past seven hundred years.

If a student from the thirteenth century suddenly found himself in a university lecture today, he would probably know immediately where he was. Even in more modern disciplines such as science and engineering, teaching methods established by Thomas Huxley in Britain and von Humbolt in Germany in the late nineteenth century—based on laboratory demonstrations and experiments—are still the standard.

All that is now under challenge. The new technologies of the Internet and multimedia are not merely enhancing the teaching and learning environment—they are fundamentally changing it. These new technologies are having as profound an impact on education as the invention of the printing press. Furthermore, these new technologies are deceptively easy for faculty to use. Consequently, change is being driven not just by government or employers, nor by university management or administration, nor by ancillary units such as the faculty development office or university multimedia centers—as in the past—but by faculty members themselves.

What Are the New Technologies?

First, we need to look at the new technologies and their impact on teaching and learning.

E-mail

Perhaps the most pervasive use of technology in higher education is using e-mail to supplement regular classroom teaching. Thus, e-mail is used not only for administrative purposes but increasingly for communication between teachers and students.

Many faculty are replacing office hours, which require a set time and place for students to contact them, with a bulletin board or e-mail service. A bulletin board enables the instructor to make announcements to all students in a class; e-mail allows for individual communication between an instructor and a student or between individual students. Some instructors have gone even further and established listserves, which enable all students and the instructor to have on-line discussions about relevant or contemporary issues associated with the course. And some instructors are allowing students to submit assignments by e-mail.

In all cases, however, these tend to be supplements to classroom teaching, although this use of technology may well replace some other activities, such as office hours or the physical delivery and collection of assignments. Still, most instructors report that this use of e-mail tends to increase rather than reduce the amount of time they spend in contact with students, which may be good for the students but can lead to work overload for instructors.

Last, in a point I will return to later, the use of e-mail requires both instructors and students to have access to e-mail, through computers and an Internet account. Without explicit policies regarding networking of instructors and students, some students may be severely disadvantaged by lack of access, as indeed may some instructors.

Presentational Software

Presentational software, such as Microsoft's PowerPoint, is another computer technology to enhance classroom teaching that is in pervasive use.

PowerPoint is a relatively easy piece of software to learn, although the skill level needed to incorporate graphics, animation, charts, video, and audio clips can escalate rapidly. Furthermore, design skills in the choice of fonts, the layout of the screen, and the use of illustration make a big difference to the quality of the presentation. It takes a little more time to prepare presentational software than a chalk-and-talk lecture, but it may in fact lead to savings in time where complex overheads or slides were previously used.

The most significant requirements are adequate training in the use of the software, a personal laptop computer for the instructor, and the provision in lecture halls of data projectors that can be quickly and easily hooked up to the instructor's laptop. These require substantial capital investment, some training, and a limited amount of technical support. Although the educational benefits of presentational software often appear obvious, they are in fact difficult to quantify.

Videoconferencing

Videoconferencing is used primarily to increase access and to make limited subject expertise available to students in a wider area.

It is particularly popular in multicampus organizations, such as state university systems in the United States. For instance, a small rural campus may have only two or three students wishing to follow a particular course. These students can be linked to a larger class in a major urban center, thus avoiding the need to hire an additional instructor.

The use of videoconferencing for the regular delivery of teaching requires a substantial investment in capital (not so much for the equipment as for room reconstruction and adaptation), investment in networks to carry the videoconferencing signals, and if several campuses are linked, expenditure on leasing or buying switching equipment.

There are several different arrangements for budgeting for videoconferencing. Sometimes departments are charged for use; at other times the service is considered free because infrastructure costs are often paid for on a statewide or institutional basis. Nevertheless, the local equipment, technical support, and preparation time of instructors are all direct costs for an institution, and the money for the infrastructure comes out of the system somewhere.

The main attraction to faculty members is that there is relatively little change in their normal teaching methods, although videoconferences generally result in more preparation time. Videoconferencing also tends to be quite stressful, particularly if the instructor tries to use interactive techniques to include remote as well as local students in discussions and class activities. The number of students per class also increases, so the amount of interactivity with an individual student tends to diminish.

Although videoconferencing may enable additional students to have access to courses in their more immediate neighborhoods, it increases instructors' workloads, adds overall cost to the system, and comes with a high marginal cost for each additional student served (see Bates, 1995).

The World Wide Web

Many instructors are now using the World Wide Web both as a presentational tool in lectures and as a means of making lecture notes conveniently available to students at other times. The World Wide Web has an additional advantage in that through Internet links instructors can access other sites from around the world and bring materials from these sites into the lecture.

Another use of the Web is to create databases of slides, photographs, and illustrations that can be drawn on for a lecture or made available to students for on-line access. By employing computer-conferencing software such as WebCT or HyperNews, the Web can also be used to create on-line discussion forums for students and instructors. Increasingly, publishers are linking texts to Web sites or even Web courses.

The disadvantage of using the Web is that it requires a special if simple computer language (HTML) to create Web pages and maintain a Web server (host computer) for the site. Although new Web-development tools and the automatic conversion of word-processed documents into HTML make it easier for subject experts to develop Web pages, other developments, such as Java programming, make it more complex.

Developing Web materials is therefore time consuming and requires either increased technical skill and preparation time from an instructor or significant technical support. Also, as use increases, the Web ideally requires a specially dedicated computer for a department and technical staff support, with both capital and operating cost implications.

Multimedia, CD-ROM

A relatively smaller number of instructors are using multimedia or CD-ROM technology to support classroom teaching. Language laboratories, computer-aided design in architecture, simulated science experiments, and large research databases containing multimedia resources such as graphics, compressed video, and audio are examples of the main uses of multimedia and CD-ROMs to support classroom teaching.

Multimedia and CD-ROMs are usually used in computer laboratories (where desktop personal computers may be networked to a local server) or on stand-alone computers using a CD-ROM. Currently, multimedia materials with video and audio clips generally require too much bandwidth for convenient delivery over public Internet systems.

There is an increasing amount of off-the-shelf software now available that can be integrated into regular classroom teaching or computer lab work. These include geographical information systems, mathematics and statistical packages, and language teaching software.

Some instructors are beginning to use multimedia to develop problem-solving and decision-making tools based on their own expertise. An experienced subject expert will enter various data and criteria necessary for problem solving and decision making into the computer database, which will also contain a large database of facts and information. The subject expert, usually working with a computer programmer, will also enter decision rules or chain decisions to certain outcomes. There may also be numerical calculations predicting, for instance, the probability of different outcomes. Students "explore" the computer environment so created and try solutions to problems and make decisions, and the computer program "predicts" the likely outcomes of their decisions based on the underlying expert system provided by the subject expert.

The development of such uses of multimedia generally requires a combination of subject expertise, computer programming, and graphics and computer interface design skills. It also requires investment in sophisticated and expensive multimedia hardware and software both for development and for student use, a high level of teaching skill, and a high level of computer expertise. Consequently, good quality multimedia learning materials are extremely expensive and time consuming to produce (on the order of $100,000 to $500,000 per CD-ROM, toward the higher end if subject expert time is included).

To justify this kind of expenditure, extensive use of the material is required and large numbers of students or clients able and willing to pay high prices for sophisticated learning materials must be found. To cover the high cost of development and to ensure widespread use of the developed materials, universities may need to form consortia to develop materials for joint use, or it may be necessary to form partnerships with private sector organizations such as publishers to share the risk.

Although the number of commercial CD-ROMs suitable for application in higher education is increasing, it is still often difficult to find the right kind of material to meet a particular instructor's needs. Consequently, the use of multimedia to support classroom teaching is still relatively low in higher education.

Approaches to the Use of Technology

There are two different approaches to the use of technology for teaching. The first is to use technology as a classroom aid; the second is to use it for distributed learning. They should be seen as two points on a continuum rather than as necessarily discrete approaches.

Classroom Aid

When technology has been introduced in the past, in the form of overhead projectors, slide shows, film, and videotapes, presentational qualities have been enhanced and students see better examples and illustrations, but the basic method of instruction is still unchanged. Rightly, such technologies have been termed *audiovisual aids,* an enhancement to but not a replacement for the basic classroom method.

One reason for the rapid take-up of newer technologies such as videoconferencing and the Web is that these have been easily integrated with traditional classroom teaching methods. No major rethinking of traditional teaching methods has been necessary. However, without changes in teaching methods, the use of technology merely adds to both the work of faculty and the study load of students. The highest cost in teaching and learning is instructor or subject expert time: Can some of that time be found by replacing or, more likely, reducing traditional activities such as lectures, laboratories, or seminars? In particular, can the teacher's role as a transmitter of information be reduced? Can the time of a teacher be concentrated on interaction with students, such as questioning, dialogue, and discussion? Can teaching be reorganized to exploit more fully the potential of the technology? For instance, statistical software can enable the instructor and students to use data sets that are more interesting and also to devote less time to calculating complex formulas and more time to interpreting results.

Distributed Learning

Distributed learning can also be seen as a continuum. At one end of the continuum, technology is used to supplement a somewhat reduced face-to-face teaching load, with significant elements of the learning conducted through the technology by learners working on their own (or in small groups around the same computer). At the other end of the continuum, learners study completely off campus (distance learning).

The Institute for Academic Technology, University of North Carolina, has provided a useful definition of distributed learning: "A distributed learning environment is a learner-centered approach to education, which integrates a number of technologies to enable opportunities for activities and interaction in both asynchronous and real-time modes. The model is based on blending a choice of appropriate technologies with aspects of campus-based delivery, open learning systems, and distance education. The approach gives instructors the flexibility to customize learning environments to meet the needs of diverse student populations, while providing both high-quality and cost-effective learning" (DEOS-L listserv, 1995).

One of the key elements of distributed learning is the use of computer communications technology as part of the teaching and learning experience. Students do not so much interact *with* the technology as *through* the technology with teachers and other learners. This can be particularly useful when the subject matter requires students to apply concepts or principles to their own context. On-line communication is also useful for areas of knowledge where there are ambiguities or where different values and interpretation are considered legitimate, and particularly for the development of collaborative learning, where students often remote from one another can work together on common tasks.

However, the main benefit of distributed learning is its flexibility and the opportunity to widen access, allowing teaching and learning to extend well beyond the campus of the university.

How Technology Is Changing Teaching

Teaching through technology can, under the right circumstances, have the following advantages over traditional classroom teaching:

• Learners are able to access high-quality teaching and learning at any time, at any place.

- Information previously available only through a professor or instructor is accessible on demand through computers and the Internet.
- Well-designed multimedia learning materials can be more effective than traditional classroom methods because students can learn more easily and more quickly through illustration, animation, different structuring of materials, and increased control of and interaction with learning materials.
- New technologies can be designed to develop and facilitate higher-order learning skills, such as problem solving, decision making, and critical thinking.
- Interaction with teachers can be structured and managed through on-line communications to provide greater access and flexibility for both students and teachers.
- Computer-mediated communication can facilitate team teaching, use of guest faculty from other institutions, and multicultural and international classes.

Consequently, new technologies are leading to major structural changes in the management and organization of teaching. These developments are increasingly being referred to in the United States and Canada as *distributed learning,* in the United Kingdom as *networked learning,* and in Australia as *flexible learning.* New technologies have the potential not only to enrich existing classrooms but, equally important, to allow institutions to reach out to new target groups, such as lifelong learners, people in the workforce, and the physically disabled.

In practical terms, we are seeing the following developments: an increase in off-campus teaching, not just for "full" distance learners who cannot access the campus at all but also for many on-campus students who find it more convenient and cheaper to study at least partly from home or the workplace; substitution in part of "real" laboratory work by computer simulations; new kinds of courses, such as certificate and diploma programs for those already graduated but needing professional updating, customized courses for specific clients such as private sector organizations, and multiple use of materials to serve different client groups, such as undergraduate students, lifelong learners, and employers; partnerships and consortia that share courses and materials to achieve economies of scale and the necessary investment to develop high-quality learning materials; and increased competition, not only from other public institutions enlarging their reach beyond state or national boundaries but also from new private sector organizations, such as the University of Phoenix on-line programs, and corporate universities.

Four Case Studies of "Transformed" Teaching

The following examples illustrate how technology changes the whole way in which teaching and learning can be organized.

Case One: Collège Boréal

Collège Boréal is a four-year-old, publicly funded college in Northern Ontario, Canada, that serves 165,000 French speakers scattered across a very large area (roughly 360,000 square miles). It has seven campuses, plus another fifteen local sites in different communities. It opened in 1995 after many years of lobbying by the French-speaking community and currently has approximately fifteen hundred full-time learners enrolled.

Collège Boréal relies on distance education technologies such as audio-conferencing, audiographics, and mostly videoconferencing for the delivery of the first year of thirty-two programs in six remote campuses. Remote learners complete half of their first-year courses in this environment, while the other half is face-to-face. For the second and third years of the program, remote learners move to the main campus. Attrition is low.

A Megastream telecommunications network has been installed to link the seven campuses through a wide area network (WAN), which includes computer-, videoconference, and telephone systems. A Virtual Resource Center and CD-ROM towers are linked to the network to facilitate access to learning materials for faculty members and learners. Across the campuses, there are about three thousand four hundred and fifty access points to the computer network and the Internet. Most classrooms have LCD projectors and document cameras installed and are fully networked, as are many public areas (including the cafeteria and the pub). Staff and learners have access to digital audio/video tools, scanners, multimedia stations, and printers. The college is now beginning to experiment with on-line courses.

On all Collège Boréal campuses and in the majority of its programs, faculty and learners use IBM ThinkPad notebook computers (laptops) as the main working tool of the institution. All full-time faculty are provided with their own notebook computers, and part-time faculty have access to notebook computers. By the year 2000, nearly all learners and all faculty will be provided with their own notebook computer. Learners pay a technological fee of $1,200 a year for their notebook computers. In addition to the computer itself, this fee covers insurance, a support and maintenance service, installation of specialized software, and access to the college intranet and to the Internet at college and from home.

The guiding philosophy is based on a learning transformation from learner dependence (where the faculty decides content and pedagogic approach), to interdependence (characterized by interaction between learners and faculty), to independence (where learners can operate on their own). The goal is learner autonomy in the workplace. This philosophy guides the implementation of any technological and academic initiatives. Laptop computers are used by learners and faculty as part of normal classroom teaching and beyond classroom walls. Learners use technology for research, electronic communications, group work, intercampus collaboration, homework, presentations, career guidance, and so forth.

La Cuisine (The Kitchen) is a physical and virtual place for the exchange of academic "recipes" and for "simmering" academic projects of a multimedia or technological nature. It is designed to meet specific needs in planning, course development, professional development, and experimentation. Faculty members come to La Cuisine for coaching, and La Cuisine provides state-of-the-art software and tools that can be used and evaluated by faculty members.

Collège Boréal has a "tech-coach" scheme to support academic staff in their use of technology. The tech-coaches are usually academic staff who have an affinity with technology. Tech-coaches help their colleagues develop their computer literacy. Through weekly workshops (three hours per week for sixteen weeks) faculty members have the opportunity to develop research, electronic communication, intercampus collaboration, presentations, multimedia productions, and also to develop operating system and software utilization skills. In Collège Boréal's first year of operation, the tech-coach–faculty ratio was 1:4 on average. The following year, tech-coaches were scaled down to one tech-coach per twenty faculty on average. Presently, there is one tech-coach for the whole college, now that faculty have become more familiar with the technology.

There are no classes between 8:00 A.M. and 11:00 A.M. on Thursdays, because this is set aside to provide guaranteed time for professional development, workshops, and meetings. Collège Boréal's Center for Information and Communication Technologies provides technical support services to the ThinkPad project, for example, troubleshooting, maintenance, and repairs. Some learners have become tutors. They are provided with basic training in peer helping and can be called upon at any time by other learners for help.

Although the college spends 2 percent of the total academic salary budget on professional development, it is funded on the same per capita basis as other colleges in the province.

Case Two: Virginia Tech

Instructors at Virginia Tech were faced with the challenge of teaching first- and second-year mathematics courses to more than seven thousand undergraduates. There was a relatively high failure rate on the traditional lecture-based courses, with substantial numbers of students having to repeat courses. By the time those students who did successfully complete the first- and second-year courses got to third- and fourth-level courses, they had often forgotten what they had learned and were unable to apply it to their current learning tasks.

Consequently, the mathematics department established the Math Emporium. This is located on one vast floor of a former discount store, and contains over five hundred computer workstations. It is open twenty-four hours a day, seven days a week, and covers the whole of the first two years' math curriculum. About 60 percent of the computer-based teaching programs were purchased off the shelf, and faculty at Virginia Tech specially developed the remaining 40 percent.

Each workstation comes with a disposable coffee cup painted red. When placed on top of a computer it means a student has a question. Patrolling instructors (some of them senior students) are available to assist the student. If the problem is more fundamental, there are cubicles around the wall of the facility where more intensive individualized instruction can be provided. Lectures are still available as an option. Thus in the Math Emporium, learners can study with a tutor, have one-on-one contact with a faculty, hear a live lecture, work in a small group, and study computer-based material.

Performance on exams has increased by 25 to 30 percent since the introduction of the Math Emporium, and third- and fourth-year students can now drop in and refresh their knowledge as and when needed.

Case Three: Universitas 21 and SEARCA

Universitas 21 is a loose consortium of twenty-one research universities, mainly from former British Commonwealth countries, such as Scotland,

England, Australia, New Zealand, Canada, Hong Kong, and Singapore. It also includes the University of Michigan. The universities of Melbourne, Queensland, and British Columbia are three Universitas 21 members. The faculties of agricultural sciences in these three universities are each having to revise completely their academic programs to meet changing needs, in terms of student demand, changing markets, and new approaches to land resource management. The three universities are also potential competitors with one another for international students in Southeast Asia.

The three universities, all of similar research and teaching status in their own countries, have decided to collaborate on the joint development of common programs in the area of land resource management. Students in each of the three institutions will have access to courses from the other two universities. In some cases, courses are being jointly developed so that they draw on the unique complementary strengths of each partner, thereby giving students access to a wider range of topics and teaching approaches.

All the courses will be available to registered students at each of the three institutions through the World Wide Web and CD-ROMs. Students are assigned to on-line discussion groups for each course, with students and instructors from each institution. They can take courses from their own institution in the regular face-to-face mode or in a distance learning mode. Approved courses from the other institutions can also be taken at a distance and transferred into their own program. Alternatively, if students can afford it, they can spend time at one or both of the other institutions, taking some courses in the program in a face-to-face mode and courses from their own university at a distance. Each university reserves the right to decide which courses from the other institutions will be accepted as part of its own program.

Two of these universities, UBC and the University of Queensland, are also associate members of the South East Asian University Consortium for Graduate Education in Agriculture and Natural Resources. This is a collection of agricultural faculties and universities committed to collaboration, and it is partially supported by funding and administrative services from the South East Asian Regional Consortium on Agriculture (SEARCA). SEARCA is a regional multigovernment organization that supports agricultural development in the Southeast Asian region. The full members of the university consortium are Universiti Gadjah Mada, Indonesia; Institut Pertainian Bogor, Indonesia; Kaesetsart University, Thailand; Universiti Putra Malaysia, Malaysia; and University of the Philippines Los Baños.

The consortium has agreed to offer a joint master's in sustainable resource management. Each institution has committed to provide at least two courses toward the program, which is focused on the needs of Southeast Asian countries for sustainable resource management. Each institution will then decide which courses it will accept into its own program. All courses will be offered in a distributed learning format for students in the other universities, and in some cases as on-campus courses for their own students or for students from other institutions who are able to travel. Each institution will award its own degree.

Case Four: University of British Columbia and Monterrey Institute of Technology

The University of British Columbia (UBC), based in Vancouver, Canada, is offering postgraduate courses over the Internet that are available not only to its on-campus master's students but also to students registered with the Monterrey Institute of Technology in Mexico (ITESM). ITESM has the rights to offer these courses in Latin America and has a side agreement to offer these courses to students at the Simon Rodriguez Experimental University in Venezuela.

The five UBC courses are integrated into ITESM's master's in educational technology (ITESM offers five more courses as part of its master's), and are available as electives within UBC's master's of education. UBC, which has the rights for the rest of the world, also offers the same courses for continuing professional education (noncredit courses) to students on a global basis. Noncredit students who take all five courses and reach a pass level obtain a postgraduate certificate of education from UBC. They can also transfer these five courses into Athabasca University's master's in distance education.

The courses are delivered using a combination of the World Wide Web, printed textbooks and articles, and satellite TV (in Latin America). Instructors from UBC are linked with students via telephone-based videoconferencing from Vancouver to Monterrey, from where the signal is uplinked via satellite to twenty-nine reception sites in Mexico and Venezuela. The same course material, assignments, and marking schemes are used for all participants, although Monterrey Institute of Technology is responsible for marking and accrediting its own students.

Teams of subject experts, instructional designers, a Webmaster, and specialists in videoconferencing, satellite TV, and graphics develop the courses. The main role of the subject experts from UBC is to research and select appropriate content, develop a Web-based course study guide, provide discussion topics, encourage and moderate student participation in on-line discussions, mark assignments, and provide feedback and guidance to learners.

Each course has between two hundred and three hundred enrollments worldwide from between fifteen and twenty countries. This program of five courses fully covers all its costs from student fees and franchises (see Bates and Escamilla, 1997, for more details), and indeed makes a small profit for UBC.

Conclusion

The examples indicate two rather different points. First, technology is being used to address weaknesses in or to provide advantages over the current conventional system of teaching in higher education. Second, the use of technology in all the chosen examples has required a major reorganization or restructuring of the conventional teaching and learning environment.

Thus, the use of technology for teaching is not just a technical issue. It raises fundamental questions about target groups, methods of teaching, priorities for funding, and above all the overall goals and purpose of a university or college. Consequently, decisions about technology need to be embedded in and subordinated to educational goals. At the same time, the educational goals themselves should take into account the new opportunities that these technologies present.

In this book, I do not question the core functions of a university or postsecondary college: teaching, research, and public service. Nor do I assume that universities and colleges should convert themselves into businesses, using technology to become financially independent of government. I passionately believe that public universities still have important social and public goals to serve.

However, the academy's core values need to be served in a rapidly changing world. Technologies now play a central role in everyone's life, and universities and colleges need to find new ways to respond to the growing demand for lifelong learning. Using technology for teaching can help universities and colleges serve the public more cost-effectively, and in particular, can prepare students better for a technologically based society.

There are also many things that are valuable in education, as in life, that technology cannot do, and this needs to be recognized.

Indeed, this book is not really aimed at those who want to ask important and justifiable questions about whether technology should or should not be used for teaching. There are others better qualified for that task (see, for instance, Postman, 1992; Noble, 1997; Feenberg, 1999).

However, whatever the philosophical arguments for or against the use of technology for teaching, improved cost-effectiveness in higher education requires more than just investment in new technologies. It will also require radical changes in teaching methods and organization. The use of technology in higher education is a Faustian contract. Dr. Faust, in Goethe's story, sold his soul to the devil for eternal life. Similarly, there is a heavy price to be paid to maximize the educational benefits of technology for teaching, a price some may feel strikes at the very soul of the academy. I will return to this in the final chapter, but in the meantime I will concentrate in the next chapters on strategies needed to support the effective use of technology for teaching and learning.

Chapter Two

Leadership, Vision, and Planning in a Post-Fordist Organization

"Healthy" institutions are "fit for purpose"; in other words, they are organized to ensure that their goals and purposes are achieved in the most effective and economical manner. The current structure and organization of most universities and colleges is largely historical and, I will argue, largely unsuited to new forms of technological delivery. If this is the case, then what models of organization can we draw from that will ensure that modern higher education institutions are fit for purpose?

Universities, colleges, and private sector organizations are in the process of introducing technology-based distributed learning and are trying to put into place support systems and management arrangements, but it is too early yet to know how successful these interventions are likely to be. Consequently, there are few examples of previously conventional higher education institutions that have significantly restructured or reorganized to ensure the successful and widespread use of technology-based distributed learning.

However, there are lessons from successful or fit for purpose organizations in other information-based sectors that we can apply to the organization and management of higher education institutions wishing to make heavy use of technology for teaching. I will examine, then, to what extent universities and colleges are—or should become—postindustrial organizations. I will then compare the features of postindustrial organizations with those of earlier forms of institutional organization, such as industrial or craft-based companies, and the implications of this for the organization and structure of universities and colleges.

As I do this, I would like you to consider the following questions:

- Need the changes be as drastic as suggested in this book? Are there not easier or less threatening ways of supporting technology-based distributed learning?
- What is the likely impact of these strategies on the "soul" of the institution? To what extent would the suggested strategies change the fundamental or core values of a higher education institution? Would such changes be good or bad, and for what reason?
- Are the proposed strategies realistic for your institution? What are the barriers to implementing such strategies? What would be needed to remove these barriers?
- Who will benefit and who will suffer as a result of such changes?
- How can universities change to meet new needs while preserving the best of the past?

Technology and the Nature of Organizations

Before putting forward various strategies for institutional change to exploit fully the potential of new technologies for teaching and learning, it is important to understand the relationship between technology and the organizational structure of institutions using technology.

Industrial or "Fordist" Organizations

Most manufacturing companies producing physical goods have until recently adopted a "Fordist" organizational model. Henry Ford, the car manufacturer, introduced or adopted a number of features of industrial organization:

- The production of uniform products
- Economies of scale (initial setup costs are high, but large volume results in each extra unit having increasingly lower marginal costs)

- Division of labor (work is broken down into different elements conducted by different classes of worker)
- Hierarchical management (decisions are made at the top, and passed down the line of command)
- Organization of people and processes into discrete, large units (divisions, for example, of manufacturing, sales-marketing, distribution, and administration), which themselves are hierarchically managed (each division with its own vice president, with departments such as accounting, payroll, personnel, each with its own level of hierarchy)
- Standardized, bureaucratic policies and procedures operating across all divisions, with a high degree of central control, often characterized by companywide collective agreements with highly organized unions, which reinforce and codify hierarchical structures and divisions within the organization.

The best examples of this kind of manufacturing organization and structure in education are the larger, national autonomous open universities in countries such as the United Kingdom, the Netherlands, Thailand, Indonesia, India, and so forth, many of which have over one hundred thousand students (what Daniel, 1998, calls *mega universities*). Organizations such as these, designed from the start as industrial models of education (Peters, 1983), are, somewhat surprisingly, not found in North America. This is due in part to the fragmented state and provincial education systems that have until now inhibited the creation of large national educational institutions.

However, there has been a rapid increase in the size and scale of conventional universities in the United States, Canada, and many other industrialized countries since the introduction in the 1960s of a mass higher education system. This has forced universities and even colleges to adopt many features of an industrialized or Fordist organizational model (see, for instance, Campion and Renner, 1992; Campion, 1995; Renner, 1995; Rumble, 1995), including large class sizes (economies of scale); a differentiation between tenured (research) professors and graduate teaching assistants, and between academic (professors), management (deans and vice presidents), and administrative staff (division of labor); hierarchical management (presidents, vice presidents, deans, heads of department), with managerial control increasingly replacing collegial decision making; large, hierarchical, and distinctly separate core organizational structures (faculties, administrative departments, buildings and plant, and so forth); and bureaucratic procedures, even—or especially—in academic areas, such as closely defined admission requirements, prerequisites, and credit banking, to ensure standardization across the organization.

Agrarian Organizations

Nevertheless, even modern universities still display many features of preindustrial or agrarian organizations. In many ways, universities and colleges are less post-Fordist and more pre-Wattist. For instance, the semester system with the long summer break reflects the origin of the land-grant universities, where students had to return home for harvesting and to tend the crops. Although the summer break provides a welcome opportunity for faculty in research universities to devote some undisturbed time to research, this hardly applies to colleges without a research mandate, yet the tradition remains.

In an agrarian society, a skilled worker was responsible for all aspects of the production, manufacturing, and distribution of a product or service. The wheelwright would collect the wood and the materials required, manufacture the wheel, and transport and market it himself. He would teach his son or a neighbor's son the same skills and the same methods. Similarly, the university or college teacher is responsible for all aspects of teaching, from selection of content and the method of teaching, to the delivery of the teaching, to the assessment of students.

Furthermore, teaching in higher education generally remains based on an apprenticeship model of handing down knowledge and teaching methods from one generation to the next. Thus a particular university subject discipline becomes a closed community, or guild, whose sole form of admission is through doctoral study managed by peers.

Post-Fordist Organizations

In contrast to both the agrarian and industrial forms of organization, information technology has led to the growth of many knowledge-based and service industries that have a very different structure from the Fordist or agrarian models. These newer forms of organization have been labeled *post-Fordist* (or postindustrial) in structure (see, for example, Farnes, 1993).

Such organizations are characterized by the following:

- Heavy dependence on information technologies (telecommunications, computers).
- Customized products and services tailored and adapted to needs of individual clients.
- Workers directly networked to clients—rapid and immediate feedback used to modify products and services.
- Workers who are encouraged to create and develop new knowledge and new ways of doing things, or who transform and modify preexisting information.
- Decentralized, empowered, creative workers, often working in teams.
- "Core" workers, who are well paid, well trained and educated, on contracts, often with ownership in the company through stock options, and highly mobile, as well as "noncore" workers and functions, who are often outsourced and lack secure conditions of employment.
- Strong leadership, characterized by clear but broad vision and objectives, and senior management, which plays an integrating, coordinating, and facilitating role.
- Often small-scale and specialist organization dependent on partnerships and alliances with other organizations with related and complementary competencies.
- Rapid development and change (post-Fordist organizations are dynamic and move very fast).
- Global operations. Postmodern industry sectors are often chaotic and characterized by new players, new amalgamations, and the unpredictable emergence of dominant technology-linked organizations.

Examples of post-Fordist organizations are Apple Computer, started originally in a garage in California; Microsoft, which has the same revenues as Sony and Honda combined but whose direct workforce is one hundred times smaller than each of those companies; and Netscape Communications Corporation, whose stock was valued at many times above the value of its physical assets, until it was bought by America Online (AOL).

Post-Fordist or Postindustrial Universities?

We have not yet seen any advanced and sustainable form of such an organization in higher education. However, elements are already visible in organizations such as the University of Phoenix's on-line programs, Nova South-Eastern University in Florida, the National Technological University based at Fort Collins, Colorado, and the Western Governors' University in the United States.

Despite its agrarian and industrial elements, certain features of a traditional university are compatible with the new post-Fordist environment. First, despite its hierarchical organizational structures, a university is in practice an extremely decentralized organization. It has a large and highly creative "core" of staff—faculty—who are able and willing to operate relatively autonomously, are concerned with the creation and transmission of knowledge, and have the power to develop and implement new ways of doing things, if they wish. Furthermore, they have a research capability that enables them to generate new knowledge in a wide range of subject areas that can be assembled and disseminated through the use of technology. Last, the better established research universities have the advantage of what marketers call a strong *brand image*.

However, the main difference between universities and colleges on the one hand and post-Fordist organizations on the other is the way one of the academy's core functions—teaching—is managed. Post-Fordist organizations are dependent on highly skilled, well-trained, and professional staff. Although university and college staff are highly skilled and (perhaps more arguably) well-trained for *research*, university and often college *teaching* is not professionalized, in the sense of being based on skills resulting from research into and analysis of teaching and learning processes. For instance, most university teaching has not been influenced to any extent by research into the psychology of learning, organizational management research, communications theories, or human-machine interaction, all of which have influenced one way or another the development of postindustrial knowledge-based organizations (see for instance, Senge, 1990). We shall see that a more professional approach to teaching will be critical for successful applications of technology to teaching.

Finally, a university or college, even a postindustrial one, is not a business. It has different functions and goals. Nevertheless, it is the ultimate knowledge-based organization, in the postindustrial sense, in that it creates and transforms knowledge. It would be surprising, then, if many lessons learned about the effective management and organization of knowledge-based businesses and industries are not also relevant to a university or college intent on using information technologies for its core function of teaching and learning. This book attempts to apply some of those lessons from other organizations, as well as lessons learned inside universities and colleges that are moving to technology-based teaching and learning.

I described in the Preface how the following strategies were identified. It is important to stress that these strategies do not result from a scientific research study but reflect the experience of many people facing similar issues in a variety of higher education institutions in the United States, Canada, and Australia.

The Importance of Leadership

The vice chancellor of one institution I visited had decided that in order to get a "virtual" university going quickly, he would set up an organizational unit totally separate from the regular campus-based operation. I suggested to him that for the university as a whole to respond to the challenge of technological change, a major *cultural* change within the staff was required, and that by creating a separate, independent organizational unit, the prevailing culture within the main university would remain untouched. His response was, "I don't have time for cultural change." Unfortunately, the widespread use of new technologies in an organization does constitute a major cultural change. Furthermore, for such change to be successful, leadership of the highest quality is required.

As we work through the different strategies, it will become clear that the effective planning and management of technology-based teaching and learning is likely to challenge many deeply held beliefs, to require changes in long-established practices, and to require the encouragement of new ways of thinking in an institution. In all the organizations I visited where technology was being used successfully for teaching, strong leadership was a critical factor. Without leadership and a strong sense of support for change in an organization, the barriers of inertia will be too great.

The good news is that effective leadership does not necessarily require someone to have heroic qualities or be an expert in the use of technology for teaching. Nor does the leadership necessarily have to come from the president or vice chancellor, and it certainly should not be leadership in the form of all the vision and strategies emanating from one person.

I will discuss later (Chapter Eight) and in more detail strategies for organizing senior management to support technological change, but effective leadership usually comes in the form of a collective approach by the whole senior management of an institution. They will share the same basic overall vision but each member of the leadership team will have a different role to play in bringing about that shared vision. Virginia Tech and Collège Boréal were particularly good examples of this among the institutions I visited. The senior management in both institutions had a shared vision and were all actively involved in supporting and facilitating the use of technology in teaching and learning, in different ways.

A senior management team, then, should either directly or through delegation:

- Define a vision for teaching and learning, and define where technology fits within that vision (see the following section for more details)
- Identify new target groups that could be reached through the use of technology
- Define priority target groups and appropriate programs for the use of technology-based delivery
- Identify areas of already-existing technology support and encourage people in those areas to provide support for "novice" technology users
- Identify areas of support outside the department, faculty, or institution, and determine the organizational and support

staffing for technology-based teaching that still needs to be provided in-house (see Chapters Five and Eight for more details)

- Ensure that innovation and the skilled use of technology for teaching is properly recognized and rewarded (see Chapter Five for more details)
- Identify the role of and priorities for face-to-face teaching in an increasingly sophisticated technology-based learning environment (see Chapter One and the following section for more details)
- Decide on key areas of investment and resource allocation for technology-based teaching (see Chapter Seven for more details).

Note that the emphasis is on helping the organizational unit as a whole to make these decisions. This may require well-tried mechanisms such as committees, task forces, and delegation. Nevertheless, leadership and a proactive approach to planning and management are essential if technology is to be used appropriately for teaching and learning.

Last, leadership is not so much a *strategy* as a *quality*. It is really the responsibility of the board of governors and the president, or deans, through their appointment processes, to ensure that senior managers or heads of department have leadership quality and an understanding of the strategic importance of applying new technologies to teaching and learning.

Vision and Strategic Planning

Developing a vision for the use of technology for teaching and learning is in my view the most important of all the strategies.

Vision

It is difficult enough for an individual to identify and describe accurately a personal vision for the future; it is even more difficult to create one for an organization as complex and diverse as a large research university. However, the journey or the process is as important as the goal (Fritz, 1989; Senge, 1990).

Visioning is a technique that allows those working in an organization to understand the full range of possibilities for teaching and learning that technology can facilitate and the possible outcomes, acceptable or otherwise, that might result from its implementation. It helps people working in an organization to identify and share certain goals. Even more important, a shared vision provides a benchmark against which to assess different strategies and actions regarding the development of teaching with technology-based teaching.

Fritz (1989) defines a vision as a set of concrete scenarios reflecting exactly what we would really like to be doing in the future. Applying this to teaching and the use of technology, the aim is to develop through a group process detailed descriptions of how an institution or department will be teaching in five years' time, and where and how technology fits into this vision of teaching and learning. The scenarios should reflect what it would be like to be teaching as a faculty member, what learning would be like for a variety of different kinds of students, and what academic and student support services would look like.

It is important that such scenarios identify ideals in concrete terms and take into account the possibilities now available through technological and other means. The aim is to develop scenarios that most faculty, students, and administrators would really want through a process, not of compromise or bargaining, but of brainstorming, persuasion, and creativity. Discussions about technology should be a key part of such a visioning process because technology can change the whole nature of the teaching and learning context.

However, technology is nested within the broader vision of teaching and learning. Technology is, by definition, a means to an end, not an end in itself. These ends or goals need to be defined in concrete terms, then the role of technology in helping to meet these ends can be more clearly understood. Indeed, the decision about whether or not to use technology in the first place should be reached through a strategic planning exercise that takes into account the overall needs of learners and the teaching goals or mission for the institution or department.

This requires some discussion about strategic planning and where visioning fits within strategic planning.

Strategic Planning

Strategic planning is a relatively well-known and standardized approach to management. Most universities have a strategic plan of one sort or another. It is usually applied at the level of the institution as a whole.

In a recent national (United States) survey, Green (1998) found that only half of higher education institutions have a strategic plan for technology. However, most of these deal with infrastructure (networks and hardware) at an institutional level (we will discuss this in more detail later in Chapter Four). Although technology infrastructure plans are essential, they are not sufficient. It is equally important to develop academic or teaching plans that specify the ways in which technology will be incorporated into teaching and learning activities. Green (1998) found that only 40 percent of higher education institutions in the United States had a curriculum or instructional plan for using technology.

Although strategic planning is usually done at an institutional level, it can also be done at a department or faculty level or by separate, semiautonomous units such as a center for educational technology or a distance education unit. Ideally, the plans for all levels should fit together and relate to one another.

The following are the traditional elements of most strategic plans:

- *Mission:* What the institution or department does, for whom, and how
- *Environmental scan:* Jargon for describing what is happening in the world around you and its likely impact on your activities; another term used is *current reality*
- *Vision:* Often confused with a mission statement; used here in a specific sense to mean a concrete description of what it would *look* like if you fully achieved what you would really like to do (no definite time scale)
- *Objectives-goals:* What you are trying to achieve, in observable terms, over the next three to five years; achievement of these goals would move you closer to the state described in the vision
- *Strategies:* Actions to achieve these goals (implementation plan)

- *Monitoring:* Ways of measuring achievements and adjusting strategies during implementation to keep on track for implementing the objectives-goals

Developing an extensive strategic plan for a large institution may be more than many senior managers want to undertake, in terms of time and money. However, the development of a detailed and clear vision for teaching and learning, especially at the level of a teaching department, is essential, whatever the commitment to other parts of the strategic planning process.

Developing a Vision at the Departmental Level

Although visioning can take place at various levels in the organization, the best place to start is at the departmental teaching level, such as English or computer sciences. Each department should be asked to develop a three- to five-year teaching plan that covers all forms of teaching, including regular face-to-face teaching, technology-based teaching, extrasessional studies (evening and weekend classes, summer schools), and "pure" distance education.

In other words, all the teaching needs of the department and the students it serves, or wishes to serve, should be addressed in an integrated way; this means relating teaching methods to the needs of different target groups, the interests and areas of expertise of the faculty, and the resources likely to be available over the three- to five-year period. In developing such a plan, it is also important to be aware of the potential for new revenue generation by using new methods and reaching new target groups.

Such a plan need not mean that tenured faculty in a department will do all the teaching; some activities may be contracted out or devolved to other units, such as continuing studies or a distance education unit, or done in partnership with external units. The teaching plan may also be different from (but might be integrated with) a plan for curriculum development and renewal. A teaching plan focuses not so much on *what* to teach, but *how.*

Any department seriously considering the use of technology for teaching and learning really needs to go through some form of planning exercise before it makes any major commitments, especially if it is recognized that technology is not just an add-on but can bring about fundamental changes in teaching. Just drifting into technology for teaching can be a dangerously expensive and ineffective policy.

Suggested steps to developing such a plan are as follows.

Developing a Strategy for Inclusion and Buy-In

No vision or plan will work without the support of faculty and students. The reason why a plan or vision needs to be developed should be explained to staff, and their maximum participation in the process should be sought.

This is not likely to be an easy task, especially in a research university. A planning or visioning process may be seen as just another exercise by the management to reduce expenditures or resources. It may be seen as diverting staff from current teaching and research activities, or it may be seen as extra load or work, especially for key participants. There may be fears that even if developed, the plan will not be implemented. And many faculty members will be concerned that it will force unwanted changes on what they do now.

However, there are counterbalancing arguments for maximum participation. The plan is likely to affect every member of the staff, so it is in everybody's interest to participate. A well-designed plan could in fact relieve current areas of concern or avoid difficulties for staff and students in the future. Teaching is a critical part of the work of the department and needs to be organized in the most effective way, so it deserves some dedicated attention. Staff and students will be able to identify their needs and influence priorities for the department. Rapid changes in the external environment, and the strategic opportunities that the use of technology present for teaching and learning, are good grounds for a department making a fundamental review of its teaching. Finally, in a rapidly changing and threatening external environment for universities and colleges, a plan offers some prospect of managing chaotic and uncertain events. The process of preparing staff for the future is probably more important than the actual details of a plan. As General Eisenhower said, "Planning is everything; the plan is nothing."

Ways should be found, through departmental meetings, subcommittees, task forces, and so forth, to involve every staff member in the department, including administrative, technical, and secretarial staff, and a wide range of students. Spreading the load can make each individual's commitment to the planning process more manageable in terms of time.

Scanning the Environment

In developing a teaching plan, staff and students will need to address some of the fundamental issues facing higher education today and how these are likely to affect their day-to-day work over the next five years.

A task group should be established to identify the external and internal environments in which the department is likely to work over the next five years. It should identify, among other things:

- The likely financial scenario over the next three to five years
- Expectations on enrollments both from the public and government and from the university or college administration
- New trends in subject matter and different approaches to teaching and learning for the key subject areas in the department
- Interdisciplinary developments, and what's happening in related departments
- The impact of technology on teaching
- The activities of potential competitors
- The department's current strengths and weaknesses (internal)
- Future opportunities and threats for the department (external)

This environmental scan can be done in a variety of ways, including brainstorming, having a small group research and write a report, inviting external speakers or consultants, and so forth. It is important, however, that the scan be done before the main visioning activity starts. It should also be done quickly, because the main trends should be relatively clear, and honestly, so that big problems or difficulties are not swept under the carpet. All those participating in the visioning process should receive a full briefing on the scan's conclusions before commencing the visioning exercise.

Developing a Vision for Teaching

Visioning provides a process and a context for involving a critical mass of people in the department in discussing the advantages and limitations of different technologies for teaching. The debate that occurs through the visioning process makes it easier to identify priorities for the use of technology and provides a basis for making difficult decisions about technology that are nevertheless likely to be supported throughout the department. One value of such a group exercise is to clarify in practical terms what colleagues mean when they talk about improving teaching and learning, or being learner-centered, or developing research skills, and so on.

The process would benefit from some preparation. Some potential activities for getting faculty to think "outside the box" are:

- Half-day workshops demonstrating innovative teaching from other organizations or related departments
- Presentations or demonstrations by outside speakers (vice president or dean, respected colleague from another institution, someone from business or industry with an outside perspective on the discipline, educational technologists, distance educators, private sector multimedia developer, World Wide Web specialist, potential student employers, students themselves, alumni, and so on)

The main purpose of such external input is to bring in new ideas or perspectives that may challenge the status quo and offer alternative approaches. The main criteria for speakers should be that they understand the subject area, have experience in using technology for teaching, or are aware of changes in the external environment that are likely to affect the department and its teaching.

The success of such a visioning process will depend on a number of factors. It will help enormously if the senior management of the institution has provided an institutional vision or context for change within which the department's vision can "nest" (see the following section).

Timing is also critical. Such a process is more likely to be valuable after a few years of experience by individual faculty in using technology for teaching on an individual basis (the Lone Ranger approach; see Chapter Three). A significant number of faculty members then will at least have some idea of the potential and limitations of new technologies for teaching.

A crisis context can also be conducive to developing radically original visions. When it becomes clear that the institution cannot continue the way it is without running into disaster, then people are willing to look seriously at alternatives just to survive. However, once a crisis exists, it may well be too late to go through a careful and thoughtful visioning process. In a crisis, decisions tend to be made on grounds other than educational benefits.

Visioning is not any easy exercise for most academics, who like to work and think at abstract or conceptual levels. Visioning depends on being very specific and concrete, so that everyone can recognize what the vision means. Also, it is extremely difficult for everyone to stop thinking about current reality or about current constraints on the unit, which, as Fritz (1989) argues, really limits thinking about the future. Current reality does have to be taken into account when one moves from vision to objectives and implementation strategies, but current reality should be cast aside when developing a vision because it will shut off too many avenues of exploration.

In many ways, the visioning process is more important than the final vision statement itself. The defined vision in fact is unlikely ever to be fully realized, or will change over time. It is primarily a process for getting staff to think seriously about and discuss teaching methods in concrete terms, and for getting them to think beyond current limitations and reality, so that quite different goals and objectives can be identified. Faculty members are understandably preoccupied with the very real and challenging day-to-day issues facing higher education institutions. A visioning process is one way to raise our heads above these daily pressures and to think about and explore the many opportunities offered by the intelligent use of technology.

Two useful references on visions for teaching and learning with technology are Conway (1998) and Noblitt (1998). To see an example of a vision statement for distributed learning developed by UBC, go to http://www.cet.ubc.ca/about/vision.html. A subcommittee of the university's Center for Educational Technology (CET) steering committee developed the vision statement. The statement includes several detailed scenarios of teaching and learning for different types of learners. The vision has several key features:

- A mix of teaching models, from programs delivered entirely in a face-to-face mode to courses available entirely at a distance

(although it was envisaged that most students would take a mix of face-to-face and technology-based teaching over the life of a full degree program)

- An increase in the provision of technology-based noncredit certificate and diploma programs, aimed particularly at mature students
- Learning materials developed as discrete modules for multiple uses (that is, the same CD-ROM might be used for on-campus and distance undergraduate students, as part of a certificate program, as continuing professional education for individuals, and as a stand-alone CD-ROM for employers or companies)
- More flexible admission and access, particularly for mature students, through the use of technology-based learning, allowing more students to be admitted to the university

It is worth noting that this vision statement, developed between 1995 and 1996, did not, as intended, go to faculties and departments for discussion and comment. This was partly because the CET steering committee felt at the time that the statement might have been too controversial or provocative and thus slowed down the adoption of new technologies. It is interesting to note, however, that in the university's new vision statement—Trek 2000, developed in 1999—many of these elements were included.

It is clearly a judgment call whether to approach the introduction of technology-based teaching on a slow, incremental, ad hoc basis, or whether to have clear long-term objectives and goals driving the use of new technologies.

Developing a Vision at the Institutional Level

The principles for developing a vision or strategic plan for a whole institution are similar to those for developing a vision for a department or faculty. However, the process is much more complex and difficult.

The most significant problem arises from the size of most universities and colleges. Once staffing exceeds one hundred, full participation becomes unrealistic. It will take too long or it will cost too much in staff time or it will result in a bland set of statements at a high level of abstraction that does not help decision making. Furthermore, involving everyone in the institution is likely to lead to a very conservative vision or plan, merely supporting the status quo.

This is where leadership becomes important. Presidents and vice presidents have a responsibility to take the long view, to respond to the pressures from society, and to think of the interests of the institution as a whole. In particular, it is important for them to recognize that technology-based teaching does not respect political or geographical boundaries. Senior management should be ahead of the faculty and the administrative staff in thinking about the future. Therefore, it is really the responsibility of the senior management team to develop a vision and a plan for the institution as a whole.

The danger of this is that the generals do not carry the troops with them. Plans come out that do not seem relevant to faculty members. Life goes on as usual. This can be avoided to some extent by encouraging departments to develop their own vision statements and plans, and by co-opting respected and influential faculty, and those who have already demonstrated innovative technology-based teaching, into the institutional visioning and planning process.

Another strategy is for the leadership to develop a draft vision or plan, then develop an extensive consultation process with the rest of the university. The danger again is that bold, innovative plans that will take an institution into new directions will be watered down and rendered meaningless by attempts to please everyone. However, consultation is not just a paper exercise; it is a form of education and awareness-raising, bringing faculty and administrators into touch with the realities of a changing world.

Finally, there must be an implementation plan, concrete actions that will take the plan and convert it to action. There are two ways to do this. The most traditional response in universities is to set up a raft of committees. Committees are useful for communication, education, consultation, recommendations, and sometimes decision making. However, in most higher education institutions committees do not execute actions. This is usually best done by individuals, or more accurately by people with the power and mandate to do things. Thus, any good implementation plan will usually indicate individuals in positions of power as being responsible for implementation of specific strategies or actions that will move the institution toward its goals and vision.

Once a strong and detailed vision statement has been developed, the process becomes more like a traditional strategic planning exercise:

- What are the likely constraints (current reality)? What funds, staffing and other resources can we mobilize? What is the best estimate of what we can achieve over the next three to five years, given the resources likely to be available and the context in which we will have to work?
- Having set a vision for the next three to five years, what are the key goals that the department or institution could possibly achieve within the next three or five years that will move us closer to our vision? (For instance, enrollments will have been increased by 15 percent, made up largely of nontraditional students who are served through technology-based learning developed for use by on-campus students as well.)
- What actions need to be taken to move toward these goals?
- What current activities could be changed or abandoned in order to meet the stated goals?
- Who will be responsible for carrying out the activities identified?
- Who will monitor progress, and how?

The last stage is critical. Someone (probably the chair of the department or his or her nominee, or a vice president at an institutional level) needs to track on a regular basis (every six months or once a year) how the plan is developing, and any adjustments to the plan should be made. If goals have been described in measurable terms, this should not be too onerous a task. Once a plan has been agreed on, it needs to be written down (or posted on the Web) and widely disseminated within the department or institution.

Plans are often developed to cover a three- or five-year period but they may be adjusted or revised on a yearly basis. Plans can be rigidly developed and followed, may be used as a rough framework for action, or may be used mainly to disseminate information and achieve consensus among key staff in an organization. Some organizations like to go through a strategic planning exercise every year, but for many this is too time consuming. A good plan should not need many significant adjustments if the scan and the visioning have been done well. One half-day meeting a year to adjust the plan may be sufficient, unless there have been major changes in the external environment.

My own preference is to develop a strong vision statement and clearly identified goals for the next few years and make sure these are widely disseminated, understood, and agreed to. I do not believe in spending a great deal of time specifying in too much detail the activities or strategies for implementing these goals, because circumstances can quickly change, and highly autonomous and intelligent faculty can often find their own ways to reach commonly agreed goals.

Limitations and Advantages of the Strategic Planning Approach

Too often strategic plans are developed but poorly disseminated to staff, forgotten about after an intense period of developing them, arbitrarily changed because of important unexpected external or internal events, or just ignored by staff.

Some argue that for organizations dependent on information technologies, strategic planning just does not work because the world moves too fast. Others find structured planning of this kind too mechanical and not sensitive enough to human factors. Another criticism is that strategic planning may work in hierarchical organizations such as the military (where it originated) and business but is unsuitable for organizations such as universities and colleges, where faculty have autonomy and independence of action. Others would argue that strategic planning is a feature of industrial organizations, unsuitable for the postindustrial knowledge-based organization (see Moran, 1998, for a more detailed discussion of the limitations of the strategic planning approach in higher education).

A Model Strategic Plan

My requirements for a "model" strategic plan for the use of technology for teaching and learning can be summarized as follows:

- The technology plan should "nest" within a wider plan for teaching and learning in a department or institution.
- The technology plan should cover both technology infrastructure *and* teaching with technology.
- The technology plan should be concrete, with a detailed vision statement, goals identified for action over the next three to five years, action steps or implementation strategies, and measurable or easily recognizable "deliverables" or outcomes, all clearly specified.

With regard to the potential impact of using technology for teaching, an institutional plan should

- Clearly identify the range of students it intends to serve, in terms of demographics, geographical location, and academic level
- Take into account the likely access to technology of its key target groups
- Define whether an institution sees itself serving primarily the needs of those in its immediate vicinity; having a state, regional, or national role, at least in some program areas; or operating on a global basis
- As a result of these decisions, indicate clearly the balance between and the different functions of face-to-face teaching and the use of technology, and campus-based and distance learning activities

These decisions will depend to some extent on the mission of an institution mandated by the government or its board. For instance, if an institution's mission is to provide universal access to all those who want or require a higher education in the state, its choice of technology for delivery will be limited by the forms of technology available to all its potential students. Requiring students to have their own computers, for instance, may disenfranchise many of those whom it has a mandate to serve.

Also, the plan should aim to exploit an institution's strengths and minimize its weaknesses. For instance, a small two-year college or a small university with limited resources will probably want to focus on local community needs and build on its close identity with the local community. Especially if it has a mandate to reach out to the disadvantaged, it may want to emphasize personal service and customize courses for local learners. This may lead it to focus on a high level of face-to-face, small-group teaching for adult basic education courses or courses aimed at minority groups. However, for some of the academic and continuing professional education programs, it may decide to bring courses in through technology from other, more prestigious institutions, adapting them to local needs and providing local tutoring and counseling.

If a university has the only medical faculty in the state, it clearly has a need not only to serve those who can attend its campus but also all those in need of continuing education. This group would include surgeons and nurses in hospitals, general practitioners, and health care workers around the state who need access to the latest research and new developments in clinical, nursing, and health care methods. Clearly, its reach should therefore be at least statewide. Technology, then, particularly for professional continuing education, is likely to play a major role in teaching in a faculty of medicine.

An important research university may see itself as operating on a global basis. Competition and collaboration are discussed as a separate strategy (Chapter Seven). However, an institution needs to consider in its vision and its strategic plan those areas where it feels it can have a global presence. It needs to ask what competitive advantage it has over local institutions in other states or countries as well as over other global competitors. What will a program from the University of Ohio mean to a student in Seattle, never mind in Karlsruhe, Germany? Why would such students want to take it? Even the most prestigious national universities will probably need to be very selective about those areas where they will "go global." Certainly, the extent to which an institution intends to operate on a global basis needs to be carefully defined in the plan.

Finally, an institution needs to define what balance it wants between face-to-face and technology-based teaching. An institution could for very good reasons decide not to go down the technology-based teaching route and place special emphasis on face-to-face and personalized teaching. Alternatively, an institution might wish to vary the degree of dependency on teaching with technology, giving more emphasis, for instance, to face-to-face teaching at the graduate level and more to teaching with technology at the undergraduate level. Other institutions may make a clear decision to emphasize the latter throughout all programs.

Many universities and colleges now have their strategic plans or technology plans posted on the Web. Here are some examples:

- http://www.mcli.dist.maricopa.edu/ocotillo/technoplan/ lists sites that contain a number of technology plans for universities and colleges in the United States.
- http://www.adm.monash.edu.au/ched/acdev.html at Monash University in Melbourne, Australia, links you to centers for teaching and learning in universities around the world.
- http://www.zdnet.com/yil/content/college/ will get you into a site that lists the one hundred most wired colleges and universities in the United States.
- http://www.umaine.edu/bearworks/default.htm will give you a detailed technology plan for University of Maine at Orono.

However, looking for plans on the Web for how an institution intends to use technology for teaching and learning is likely to be a time-consuming and frustrating experience. Many of these sites do have mission statements, general strategic plans for the institution as a whole, and often detailed technology plans. However, few sites provide detailed *academic* plans that provide information on teaching and learning goals and strategies for using technology. Institutions will need to address this gap if they are to justify their already large investment in technological infrastructure and support systems.

Conclusion

A plan will be only as good as the vision that drives it. In my visits to universities, I saw no lack of commitment by senior managers to investing in technology for teaching and, indeed, no lack of imagination on the part of many faculty members about how technology could be used to improve the quality of learning. What often is lacking is *strategic* vision, that is, how technology can be used to change the way a university or college does its core activities or business so that it can reach out to new needs and new target groups. This is where a well-developed visioning process can be most valuable, and this is the challenge for the senior management in particular.

Chapter Three

Planning and Managing Courses and Programs

In this chapter, I want to look at the planning and management of technology-based teaching and learning at the course or program level.

Laissez-Faire Planning, Lone Rangers, and the Autonomy of the Faculty

The ease of use or "transparency" of technologies such as the World Wide Web and videoconferencing makes it much easier than in the past for faculty to develop technology-based learning materials and course delivery. The World Wide Web, for example, allows a teacher easily to adapt materials created for lecture or classroom use and present them as attractive color graphics and text. Once the materials are created as Web pages, it is a simple matter to make them available for off-campus as well as on-campus students.

In most countries, tenured faculty have considerable autonomy with regard to teaching. Especially in research universities, there is a long history of faculty writing grant proposals for research purposes, and this model has been extended to cover innovative approaches to teaching. Consequently, the most common approach to encouraging the use of technology, at least in universities in the United States and Canada, has been to provide individual faculty members with small grants that provide funding for a part-time graduate student and some equipment or software.

Thus, technology-based materials are increasingly being initiated and developed by faculty through what I call the Lone Ranger and Tonto approach. Tonto is the computer-skilled graduate student who does the HTML markup and scanning and generally tries to keep the professor out of technical trouble.

Advantages of the Lone Ranger Model

Using small grants to encourage faculty to use technology has several advantages. It can get a wide range of faculty started on using new technologies for the first time. It provides opportunity for experiment and the development of faculty skills in using technologies. It can help faculty understand the potential of the technology and thus lead to innovative ideas about how to use the technology in a specific subject area. It allows graduate students to develop computer skills that can be applied to their area of subject expertise. It avoids having to make difficult decisions about long-term investment in technologies that may prove ephemeral; "winners" can emerge. Finally, it maintains the autonomy of faculty to decide on the teaching method that best suits them, thus fitting in with the prevailing university and college culture.

Using grant monies to support individual proposals from faculty could be considered a laissez-faire, or bottom-up, approach to planning, compared with strategic investment, or a top-down approach. A laissez-faire strategy creates an environment that encourages experimentation. From a management perspective, it also enables successful practice to be identified from the bottom up and the resources needed to support such innovations to be more easily identified. Faculty are likely to support a policy of using central funds to provide technical support to individual professors. As already noted, a laissez-faire approach fits well with the culture of universities and colleges, where faculty have considerable autonomy and are used to operating on a small-grant basis for research.

Disadvantages of the Lone Ranger Model

There are also many disadvantages to this approach. On most university and college campuses, as a result of Lone Ranger funding models and laissez-faire approaches to the use of technology for teaching and learning, amateurism rules in the design and production of educational materials.

Standard classroom materials, such as lecture notes, may be carried across to a Web site without being adapted to the requirements of the medium. More important, the many unique features of the technology, such as links to other sites or the opportunity for students to add their own contributions to the site, may not be exploited.

A characteristic of many Lone Ranger projects is that often there is never a final product. The site is constantly under construction or not developed as a full teaching resource available on a regular and reliable basis. This is because the project drags on, being constantly upgraded or improved, or has to be redesigned as a result of inappropriate or outdated technology decisions in the early stages. The initial funding is often inadequate to complete the job, and much effort is spent seeking additional funding to continue the project.

Often the graphics and the interface are poor compared with commercial products with which students are familiar, and the potential for high-quality learner interaction with the materials and other students is often missed. Finished products have limited applicability because their graphics and interface are not of high enough quality or because they are insufficient in volume to become commercial products or be used by other teachers in the department.

The most valuable resource in a university or college is the time of a professor. The problem with Lone Rangers is that they often spend a lot of time doing technical work, such as designing Web pages or animation, that a professional could do much more quickly and much more effectively. The prima donna shouldn't paint the scenery.

Even when a product is finished, no thought may have been given as to how the material will be used. It may be restricted to being a supplement to an individual professor's teaching when it could be used as a general resource for the department or faculty or the university as a whole. For instance, in many universities similar courses with common "core" content are offered in a variety of different programs, each with its own teacher. Thus, the same basic statistical techniques may be used in psychology, sociology, plant sciences, geography, political science, and so forth. A common statistical teaching package could be designed in such a way that it could easily be customized for other departments. Developing "core" materials with several applications, however, needs a more strategic approach to materials development. Teachers from several disciplines or departments need to be involved in the design to ensure application and use of the core materials in all relevant areas. Consequently, a feature of many Lone Ranger projects is that technology applications end up being a costly supplement to conventional teaching, merely increasing the instructors' (and students') workload. The result is an increase in the institution's overall unit costs.

For the extra cost of using technology to be justified, it needs to be accompanied by the reorganization of the teaching process. This requires moving away from fixed, scheduled group instruction to more flexible and individualized modes of learning, and to more strategic use of the materials, in order to support a variety of teaching and learning contexts.

Another disadvantage of the Lone Ranger approach is that dissemination of knowledge gained from the experience is often poor or haphazard. Only "successful" projects get known, and even then the practices that led to success may not be shared. Unsuccessful projects just fade away, and equally important lessons about how *not* to do things are lost. Therefore, other projects that fall into the same traps continue to get funded.

In addition, it is very difficult to identify the level of funding required to support a laissez-faire approach. Any funding agency knows that whatever the budget available, there will always be enough applicants to use that money. Without some strong criteria based on knowledge and experience about the requirements of successful projects, there is no way to make valid judgements about projects. Consequently, poor projects may get funded just because the proposer is generally good at grant proposals or can tell a good story.

There is even the issue of how to deal with a really *successful* Lone Ranger project. Funded as a separate, self-contained activity with limited funds and timetable, what does the institution do if the project turns out to be highly successful? This may seem to be a good problem to have, but in fact there may be significant difficulties in scaling up the project as well as resistance from other instructors who were not a part of it. For large-scale implementation a major effort may be needed to reallocate funds and make many organizational and institutional changes that were not foreseen when the project was set up. A policy based on short-term grants can be seen as "funding for failure," because there is no strategy for dealing with successful projects. Failure is actually a relief, because the organization does not have to do anything more.

Improving the Lone Ranger Model

Despite the rather chaotic and hazardous nature of the laissez-faire approach, it has strong support in many institutions. Supporters argue that new technologies are a new field for teaching; it is not clear yet what works and what does not; and in an argument heard especially in research institutions, the best way to learn how to use these new technologies is to experiment with them. Faculty are considered to be professionals, capable of making their own decisions about what help or training they need, and they should be trusted to use the grants wisely. If the necessary technology is provided, highly able subject experts will work out the best way to exploit it for teaching.

There are, of course, many ways in which the Lone Ranger model could be strengthened so that better-quality results are achieved. Here are some suggestions:

- Before funding, require the grant applicant to specify how the material will be used once the project is completed.
- Require matching funds from the department or faculty; this is a good test of departmental or faculty commitment to the project.
- Require the grant holder to attend (or to have attended) a short training course on multimedia or Web design as a condition of the grant.
- Require "show and tell" sessions where faculty bring along their projects at various stages of development for feedback and comment, and make someone responsible for organizing these sessions on a regular basis.
- Offer workshops, face-to-face or on-line, or contract in external agencies to train faculty to use the new technologies; give funding priority to those who have been through such courses.

- Require a formal evaluation consisting of both student feed-back and the sponsor's own experience, including disadvantages or negative experiences, and make sure the project is adequately funded to do this; this enables the funding committee also to learn from experience.
- Create a central technical support unit (either in a faculty or for the institution as a whole, depending on size) with graphics, interface, and instructional designers who can be called on for assistance when needed (see Chapter Eight).
- Establish a showcase drop-in center where staff can go to get help and develop materials.
- Hold back 20 percent of the grant from the faculty member until the work is almost completed; the 20 percent is released on successful demonstration to the funding committee of the teaching materials created.

There are probably many other ways to improve Lone Ranger projects. However, the level of administrative support and hence cost to the organization increases as the list develops. Furthermore, this is still generally a laissez-faire approach. It depends on the faculty member being willing to get help. There is no guarantee that these services to instructors, even if provided, will be used, or even if used, will be of sufficient depth or intensity to lead to real improvements in the quality of the material produced. Staff who most need help may not seek it.

Achieving Quality in Technology-Based Teaching and Learning

For most universities and colleges, quality teaching and learning is of paramount importance, at least in terms of their stated goals. Quality is a mantra that is easy to chant but more difficult to implement. However, it will become increasingly important for universities and colleges to achieve high quality in any technology-based teaching and learning materials and programs that they develop.

Once materials are created on the Web, the potential student base becomes global. At the same time, many other institutions are also going in this direction and will be able to offer their courses and programs to your institution's traditional students. In an increasingly competitive environment, the organizations that will survive—as is the case with any of the other new knowledge-based industries—will be those that provide services that the public values at a better price and quality than the competition.

Aspects of Quality

There are several components of quality in technology-based educational materials.

Content

The brand image and the research capability of an organization become critical here. Is this unique or valuable teaching material for which there is a need or demand? Quality of content is not usually an issue in most research universities, but it may be in smaller universities and in colleges that have no research mandate.

Media Production

Are the graphics clear and well designed? Are the screens easy to read? Are the sound and video easy to hear and see? Are the unique features of each medium (video, audio, text, computing) fully exploited? Is the material well assembled and structured? Is the screen designed in such a way that students intuitively understand the range of activities open to them and how to accomplish them, and is the interface designed so that they can easily find all the material they need and move around the teaching materials easily?

Instructional Design

Are the learning objectives clear? Does the material result in the desired learning outcomes? Does it have the appropriate mix of media to achieve the learning outcomes in the most efficient manner? What is the quality and nature of the interaction between student and learning materials? What is the role of the tutor-instructor relative to the technology-based learning materials? Are the materials coherently structured?

Delivery and Student Support

Are materials ready and delivered on time? Does the student have to develop new skills or buy extra equipment or download new software to use the learning materials? How quickly can the materials be downloaded over public networks? What happens if students have technical problems? Can learners ask questions or discuss materials with other students? Who gives feedback? At what times is help available? How will tutoring and assignment marking be organized? Who is responsible for hiring additional tutors and paying them?

These issues all need to be addressed to ensure high-quality teaching and learning through the new interactive learning technologies. We shall see in the following paragraphs that project management rather than a Lone Ranger approach offers a better chance of achieving high quality.

The Importance of Timing

Certainly, there is a time in an organization when the laissez-faire or Lone Ranger approach may be suitable, and that is when a university or college is just beginning to commit to the use of new technologies. A laissez-faire approach combined with some cash grants spread evenly across the institution is a reasonable and often effective means of gaining buy-in from faculty and helping them understand the potential and requirements of using new technologies for teaching.

However, I believe that the laissez-faire approach is not a sustainable way to run an organization that has made a fundamental commitment to using technology for teaching. It is too hit-and-miss. It wastes resources, ignores the experience and many lessons that have been learned outside the higher education sector about how to design and develop creative media products and services, and above all fails to ensure high-quality technology-based teaching in any consistent or widespread form. We need therefore to look at a more systematic approach for the development of high-quality technology-based distributed learning.

The Project Management Approach

One way to ensure high-quality cost-effective technology-based teaching and learning is through *project management*. Project management is used extensively in other creative multimedia areas, such as filmmaking, advertising, and video and computer games, and also in many engineering and technology-based projects.

A project may be a full program of courses, an individual course, a research study, or a small module, such as a CD-ROM or Web site, located in a larger unit of teaching such as a face-to-face course. Face-to-face courses could be considered projects alongside distributed learning or distance education courses. Alternatively, a project may be handled differently from the rest of the teaching, particularly if it is an experiment or an innovation to be tested. Resources sufficient just for that project would then be allocated.

The Project Management Process

There are many models and approaches to project management (see Ross, 1991, for one common approach). What they all share is that project development and delivery involves a team of individuals each contributing different skills, and the process is managed by a team leader or project manager.

What defines a project is the process used to manage it. It has a defined set of resources, usually determined at the outset of the project, a time line, and a clear "deliverable" in that it is clear what the project has to achieve and it is obvious when it is completed.

As already stated, academics are expected to work in a team with a project manager and others with specialist skills. The project manager need not be the senior academic or instructor. It is best if the project manager is someone trained in project management techniques. Indeed, there are advantages to the instructor not being a project manager because much of the project manager's role is administrative and bureaucratic.

In the approach taken by the Open University in Britain, there is a chair of the course team, who is the senior academic, and a course manager, who is an administrator, and in effect, the project manager. In addition, the team also includes an educational technologist (instructional designer), a print editor, a BBC producer (if there is a television or radio component), and if there is a computing component someone from the academic computing area. All the core academic and teaching decisions are made by the team as a whole, who may or may not be heavily influenced by the chair, but in practice the academics in the team in the end make the final decisions.

The Open University model, especially for interdisciplinary courses such as foundation courses, often involves a large team of sometimes thirty people or more. They often meet on a regular two-weekly basis. All materials in theory need to come to the team for approval, and print-based materials may go through three different drafts before finally being approved. This is a very time-consuming and expensive development process (hence the term *industrial*) and can be only justified by the very large numbers of students who take Open University courses (for instance, the science foundation course will be taken by thirty thousand students or more).

The project management approach in institutions such as UBC, which offer courses both on campus and for distance education students, tends to be a more streamlined and flexible version of the Open University model. At the Distance Education and Technology unit (DE&T) at UBC, we usually combine instructional design and project management in a position called *course developer*, although for some projects a faculty member may be the project manager. The DE&T course developer will work closely with a single academic or subject expert. However, depending on the overall design, the course developer will be able to draw on other specialists within and outside the unit, such as a Web programmer, librarian, graphics designer, interface designer, video producer, and multimedia developer.

All the participants in the process may meet as a team at the beginning of a project to establish an overall design, which may result in a "template," such as a particular look and design for a Web site. From then on, the subject expert will generally work on developing the academic content and the course developer will then convert this into a technology-based format, in consultation with the subject expert and drawing on specialist technical support as needed.

The project management approach to developing and delivering technology-based teaching and learning ensures that resources are used efficiently and that individual team members contribute appropriate skills and knowledge to the project.

Project Management and Resource Management

Project management works best when it is tied to resource allocation. Resources include staff, facilities, and money. A whole department could be organized on a project management basis in that all the resources available to a department are pooled and then allocated to projects. Resource allocation can be tied to project management. In other words, a condition of receiving funds or the allocation of staff to work on a project is that they all agree to work to a project management model.

Resources for projects may come in the form of funds held back centrally to promote innovation or earmarked for distributed learning or distance education projects. Individual faculty members or departments submit proposals to a committee or senior manager who then allocates funds according to the merits of the proposals. Resources allocated may include cash for backfilling or buying out faculty to work on a project, as well as cash for materials purchase and distribution. It may also include the allocation of staff time for those in regular employment, or cash may be used to contract in work. At DE&T, our course developers and our other support staff are funded from a central distance education fund and have regular management and professional positions. Each year their time (usually in days) is allocated to projects through a process set up to allocate resources to project proposals.

Developing Project Proposals

To determine the resources needed for a project—including the time of course developers and other production specialists—at DE&T we have introduced an extensive project proposal development process. This means establishing each course or teaching module as a project, with the following elements:

• A fully costed proposal that identifies the number and type of learners to be targeted (and in particular their likely access to technology); clearly defines teaching objectives; chooses technologies; and carefully estimates budget allocation (including staff time, copyright clearance, use of "fixed" media

production resources, such as video compression, as well as actual cash)
- A team approach involving any combination of subject experts or faculty, project manager, instructional designer, graphics designer, computer interface designer, desktop editor, Internet specialist, and media producer, depending on the design of the project
- An unambiguous definition of intellectual property rights
- A clear agreement on the flow of revenues, such as student tuition fees, sales of materials, and revenue sharing arrangements
- A plan for integration with or substitution for face-to-face teaching
- A production schedule with clearly defined milestones or deadlines, and a targeted start date
- An agreed process for evaluation and course revision and maintenance
- A defined "life" of a project before redesign or withdrawal of the course

At DE&T, a project is not defined in one step. We have a five-stage approach to project definition. Following an invitation to all faculties to bid for funds, a department or individual academic is invited to submit a short proposal (usually two to four pages) requesting funds or assistance. We provide a short questionnaire to help faculty at this stage.

One of our senior staff then works with the lead academic to develop a fully costed proposal. This is a critical stage in the process, where course objectives and teaching methods are clarified, alternative modes of delivery are explored, and the resources that will be necessary to implement the proposal are identified. The proposal has to be signed off by the head of department and by the dean, to ensure that the proposal fits in with Faculty and departmental priorities.

The project proposal then goes to a universitywide committee of academics for adjudication. Each proposal is in competition with all the other proposals for distance education funding. A set of criteria for selection has been developed, including the number of students to be served, strategic positioning, innovation, potential for revenue generation, and so forth.

Following allocation of funds, a detailed letter of agreement is drawn up between the academic department and DE&T, which clearly sets out responsibilities on both sides, and ties down production schedules, intellectual property, sharing of revenues, and so forth. Once the project is funded, DE&T managers track progress, schedules are rearranged to take account of changing circumstances, and budgets are sometimes changed (but more likely rearranged) as a result, all by mutual agreement with the academic department.

The last stage is to draw up an annual account of progress. This will describe:

- The number of projects in production in any one year
- The number of projects completed in any one year
- Funds disbursed against funds allocated for each project (so unspent funds can be reallocated)
- Dates of courses first offered during the year
- Enrollments for each new course, and for all courses combined

This last stage provides a measure of accountability for the DE&T unit and for the disbursement of development funds. Final evaluation of each project is a separate but equally important process. Details of this process, including questionnaire and sample proposals and letters of agreement, can be seen at http://det.cstudies.ubc.ca/devman/. The information available at this site includes:

- Criteria for funding projects
- Terms of reference and membership of the advisory committee on distance education (which allocates resources)
- Memo inviting project proposals
- Questionnaire to be filled in by proposer
- Example of a proposal for an undergraduate credit DE course (nursing)
- Example of a letter of agreement (nursing)

- Example of a proposal for a noncredit continuing education proposal (pharmaceutical sciences)
- Example of a letter of agreement for a noncredit continuing education proposal (pharmaceutical sciences)
- Sample project schedule
- Example of calculating costs and revenues for a self-financing Web-based course

Although this process has been developed for distance learning courses and programs, it can just as easily be applied to on-campus uses of technology for teaching and learning.

Disadvantages of the Project Management Approach

The biggest problem with this approach is that it is often alien to academic environments, where teachers and instructors are used to working as autonomous individuals, especially with regard to their teaching. The project management approach is often seen as a bureaucratic, expensive, and unnecessarily complicated process, and a process that restricts the freedom and autonomy of the teacher.

Others (for example, Wilson and Cervero, 1997) criticize the "technico-logical" approach to planning and management inherent in project management. They argue that as far as education is concerned, this logical approach to planning and management just does not work. Life is too complex to be controlled in this way, and such approaches restrict originality and creativity.

There is certainly a danger in the rigid application of project management models. Some approaches, such as the network phase model proposed by Ross (1991), can be extremely detailed and time consuming. They treat the management of course development in much the same way as one would manage the construction of a building or the production of automobiles. But in course development, resources, particularly human resources, cannot be allocated and managed as mechanistically as they can in a production plant or on a construction project. The project manager often has only limited authority over key team members, particularly the faculty members. Thus, well-planned production schedules, more often than not, fall by the wayside.

This does not mean though that project management should be abandoned. It just means one has to be realistic about what can be accomplished and be prepared to make modifications along the way. At the DE&T unit at UBC we have found it more useful to use a much looser project management approach that specifies responsibilities and completion dates but does not attempt to quantify every activity and phase, nor to schedule activities or resources on a microlevel. The project manager and the academic have a good deal of freedom to move resources around and adjust schedules to meet the reality of academic life.

However, at the end of the day, there still has to be a course developed and deadlines met. Our agreement does give DE&T the right to withdraw from a project and reallocate resources, if:

• The project gets more than three months behind schedule.
• The project is developing in a way that was not planned or agreed.
• The project is going well over budget.

We try to avoid this situation arising in the first place. However, on the few occasions when we have had to resort to canceling a project, this has been received with some relief. The subject expert is relieved because of being overcommitted and unable to get the work done in time, and the head of department is relieved because of concerns about the impact of the project on the rest of the department's teaching and research activities.

It still takes between four and six months to negotiate from initial interest to release of funds and resources. However, once a letter of agreement is in place this process speeds up production. It avoids long and protracted arguments over rights, revenue sharing, and responsibilities, and it provides a clear framework for the work of the project team. It is particularly important for multimedia projects because it provides boundaries and control around activities that otherwise can easily get out of hand in time and cost. Most important of all, a project management approach allows the costs of different kinds of projects to be tracked, enabling judgments to be made regarding the cost-effectiveness of different approaches.

From the outside the project management model may appear more expensive, but one has to look at benefits as well as costs. At

UBC we have spent several millions of dollars on Lone Ranger projects over the last five years. Although this has been extremely useful for faculty development and kindling an interest in using technology for teaching, the results as far as impact on the regular teaching of the university have been very limited. The most valuable output to date of the Lone Ranger funding in fact has not been teaching materials but the development of Web course development software, in the form of WebCT.

The last criticism of the project management model is that it inhibits creativity and reflects an industrial rather than a postindustrial model of management. However, project management is a primary and essential mechanism in most postindustrial organizations, such as software development companies, video and computer games companies, and multimedia production companies. It does decentralize the production process and it gives control to a team of creative people. There are many forms of creativity required for high-quality multimedia teaching and learning, and the subject expert has the necessary knowledge and skills in only some areas of this process. The project team allows for the integration of a wide range of creative skills.

Finally, I have to say that we have found that most of the academics we have worked with in a project management model really like it. It takes from them many of the tasks they neither enjoy nor wish to do and it provides a clear framework and role definition, which enables them to keep their work for the project under control.

Conclusion

Course development tools such as WebCT, Learning Space, and Blackboard counter some of the weaknesses of the Lone Ranger approach by building in instructional design features. However, the course development tool is only a part of the teaching process. It has to be integrated into a system that includes student support, assessment and accreditation, and above all, tutoring.

There is then a continuum in the use of technology for teaching. At one end is the use of technology as an audiovisual aid in the otherwise conventional classroom. This is by far the most common use of the new technologies to date; for this, the Lone Ranger model is perfectly adequate, provided one is willing to live with the extra time demanded of the professor.

The next point on the continuum is the use of technology in a mixed mode, where flexible access to technology-based learning materials is combined with (reduced) classroom teaching. The Lone Ranger model may work well here if material developed elsewhere is accessed or brought in, if new material development is relatively minor, or if off-the-shelf course development tools such as WebCT, Learning Space, or Blackboard are used. However, a project management model would probably be better here, especially for dealing with issues such as copyright and student support.

The third point in the continuum is the development of a program totally delivered at a distance to individual learners. Finally, there is the development of a major multimedia project, such as an expert system or a whole set of courses delivered by CD-ROM and the Internet. For these situations, project management is essential.

In the end, the best use of technology occurs when the academic not only has a deep understanding of the subject but also has an imagination and a vision of how the subject could be taught differently with new technologies. This can be found both in Lone Ranger and project management models. Nevertheless, a project team, with specialists with an understanding of the possibilities of new media, can help stimulate an academic to develop such a vision. More important, the project management model provides the essential support and creativity in production and delivery to bring such a vision to fulfillment in a timely and cost-effective manner.

Chapter Four

Technology Infrastructure and Student Access

The first strategy many institutions adopt is to put in place the technology infrastructure. Although this is an important strategy, it needs to be linked closely with other strategies.

What Is Technology Infrastructure?

Technology infrastructure has several elements.

Physical Infrastructure

The physical infrastructure includes desktop or laptop machines and mainframes or servers that are linked to desktop machines. It also includes the physical network (cables and wires, fiber and Ethernet) that connects all the machines, and the operating software and routers that enable the machines and networks to work. Infrastructure can also include telecommunications links to the world outside the campus, and between campuses, including telephone services, videoconferencing equipment and networks, and of course access to the Internet.

Large research universities such as UBC may need to spend up to $4 million to $5 million a year to develop and maintain the necessary campus technology infrastructure, high-speed networks that link every building and every classroom and office within every building. Many faculty and staff members may not have a computer or know how to use one. Many universities and colleges may have old buildings without adequate conduits for wiring, or asbestos fillings inside walls that need to be removed before modern cabling can be installed. Servers may need to be installed in each department or networked to other servers on campus. Once networks are installed, equipment and software need to be continually upgraded because of the rapid rate of technological development in information technologies, which shows no sign of abating.

Internet connections with the outside world need to be established, and ports and other communications facilities need to be installed to provide students in residences, off campus, or at satellite campuses and other institutions with access to the main university computer network.

Human Support for Infrastructure

Even more important than the physical infrastructure are the people required to make the physical infrastructure work. These staff members are also part of the technology infrastructure. They may work in a central unit or in a faculty or department to support local needs.

There are in fact four levels of human support required to exploit technology to the full. The most obvious and basic are the technical support people who are needed to ensure that the networks and equipment are properly installed, operated, updated, and maintained. I describe them as the *technology infrastructure support staff*.

At the second level is the media production and services staff, such as interface designers, graphics designers, videoconferencing managers, or graduate students who do HTML markup. They support the creation and application of educational materials and programs using technology. I describe them as the *educational technology support staff*. Technology infrastructure staff will be needed whether or not technology is used for teaching; however, the educational technology support staff are needed only if or when technology is to be used for teaching.

At the third level are those who provide educational services and expertise, such as instructional design, faculty development, project management, and evaluation, to support the use of technology for teaching. I describe them as the *instructional design staff*.

The fourth level is made up of the professors, instructors, teachers or subject matter experts who create content and provide the teaching over the networks and infrastructure. I describe them as the *subject experts*.

Although the latter two groups are not critical elements of the technology infrastructure, they are essential for the creation and delivery of high-quality technology-based teaching.

Funding the Technology Infrastructure

Physical infrastructure, such as networks and major equipment purchases, is often seen as a once-only investment and hence is usually funded from capital budgets. However, rapid advances in technology and the need continually to replace or update networks and equipment makes this a dangerous assumption. In contrast, the cost of the technology support staff is recurrent—that is, has to be found each year—and hence tends to be treated as part of the base operating budget.

Thus, physical infrastructure is less likely to compete for funds that directly affect teaching, such as the general purpose operating fund, whereas the cost of support staff directly competes with funds for teaching and research. Consequently, the human technology support side is often underfunded. This may explain why the most consistent complaint across universities and colleges from those responsible for technology applications is the inadequacy of resources for human technical support for technology, a point I will return to later.

Farther down the chain, from technological support to educational technology support, it becomes even more difficult to secure adequate resources. If the network crashes, its impact is obvious; the value of an instructional designer is much harder to justify when funds are tight. Nevertheless, from a teaching and learning perspective, it is critical that academics and instructors receive the training and educational support needed, an issue discussed more fully in Chapter Five.

Finally, the most expensive link in the chain is the faculty themselves. Without their time and energy no teaching or educational materials will be developed and distributed across the infrastructure.

It is essential, of course, to have a strategy for developing the technology infrastructure of a university. Priorities must be set on both the level of investment and the areas of investment. In particular, the right balance has to be struck between capital and recurring costs, and between physical infrastructure and human support.

Assessing the Adequacy of the Technology Infrastructure

In your own institution, how adequate is the technology infrastructure? Does every faculty member have a desktop or laptop computer? How modern are these machines? How many classrooms have Internet access, computers, and projectors that can display computer-generated information, or plug-in ports and power for student portable computers? What is the ratio of computers in labs to students in the department? How obsolete is the hardware and software in the labs?

Is every building and office networked? Does everyone have Internet access? How fast is the network to the desktop? How many ports or lines are there for external Internet access? How long does it take to get connected from outside the institution? Does the university or college provide its own Internet service for students and staff? If so, how is this paid for? Does the institution have wideband networks across campus, and are these networks adequately connected to the external world?

How many centers or locations are there for videoconferencing, or is it all in one location on campus? (Note that the more centralized, the less likely it is to be used.) Are all satellite campuses as well served when it comes to infrastructure as the main campus? Are they all linked within a common telecommunications network? How integrated are the communications? For instance, is the telephone system physically separate from computer communications and from videoconferencing? Or can the network handle all services digitally and in an integrated way?

Does your institution actually know the answer to these questions? Is anyone responsible for monitoring the overall provision of technology across the institution?

Does your institution have useful academic and administrative functions available through computers that would make the job of the average faculty member easier (for example, e-mail, access to departmental financial information, student records, and the Internet)? You can be sure that if many faculty members do not have computers or do have computers but no useful services available to them, they are not likely to use computers for teaching purposes either. Is there any training for faculty or students on how to use their computers or the Internet? How easy is it to get this training?

These are all useful standards for the technological infrastructure of an institution. Many of these would be worthwhile whether or not there is an academic plan for the use of technology for teaching. However, the cost of achieving these standards is likely to be huge. At UBC, the aim is to spend approximately $4 million a year over five years in further developing the infrastructure, in addition to the costs of maintaining current operations. This will have to continue beyond a five-year period because the technology continues to change rapidly. In such a scenario, then, it is essential to ensure that investment in infrastructure is balanced by investment in applications. It is not so much the *direction* of the development of technology infrastructure that will be influenced by academic planning as the *speed* of development and the priorities for investment.

Relationship Between Technology Infrastructure and Academic Planning

Although a technology infrastructure strategy is absolutely essential, unfortunately it is often the first—and sometimes the only—strategy adopted by universities and colleges, a kind of "build it and they will come" attitude. Many university and college managers believe that putting in the latest and most advanced technologies, and providing access to this technology to all parts of the university or college community, will automatically result in innovative teaching applications.

This thinking is encouraged by the multiple applications for information technologies—such as administration and communications as well as teaching—that make relating costs to benefits extremely difficult because the benefits are so diffuse. It is also driven by a wish to keep up with the Joneses. Nothing causes a president to panic more than the knowledge that the main competitor across the state has just installed a fiber-optic network on campus and intends to go global. Furthermore, the fact that most technology investment is seen as a once-only capital investment, often from a separate state budget, means that the investment can be made apparently without affecting annual operating budgets.

However, the track history of technology investment in universities and colleges suggests that merely putting in the technology is no guarantee of its use. Universities and colleges are full of equipment stored in cupboards and empty studios and production facilities from previous waves of technology investment. Furthermore, it is a dangerous fallacy to assume that capital investment will have no impact on recurrent operating expenditure. Usually, the annual operating costs of managing and servicing technology infrastructure investment will exceed within the first year the capital investment cost, or the technology will just not function effectively. If the costs of technology applications, such as data entry and analysis, and the development of technology-based teaching and learning are included, then for every dollar spent on infrastructure, somewhere in the order of $10 will need to be spent on support and applications. Physical infrastructure is an important part—but only a part—of a much wider system, all parts of which need to be adequately funded.

Although technology infrastructure has to serve administrative and communication needs as well as academic needs, the technology infrastructure plan should be at least partly driven by the university's overall vision and strategy for its teaching. Because these days most universities and colleges either have or should have a technology plan, you might like to find the answers to the following questions for your own institution:

1. Who wrote the plan? Who was chair of the committee? An academic? A technology person? An administrator? What was (or is) the balance of the committee across these three areas? Who was driving the plan: the academics, the technology people, or the administrators (registrar, bursar, and so on)?
2. Is the plan integrated within a general strategic plan for the institution or does it stand alone?
3. Are there any explicit links between the technology infrastructure and educational goals and purposes? How specific

are these? Is it clear what specific learning outcomes or strategic institutional goals will result from the implementation of the technology plan? Is it clear why investment in technology would result in these goals, or could these goals be achieved in other, less expensive ways?

4. In your institution, how well defined are the academic plans for the application of technology for teaching and learning? To what extent if any are academic plans driving decisions about investment in technology infrastructure in your institution? Who is responsible for setting academic priorities in this area? Can you find any academic or teaching plan that matches or integrates with the technology plan?

5. Is it really possible for a big research university—as distinct from a small college—to develop a plan or set of *academic* priorities that could influence investment in technology infrastructure? Is it too large and diverse, or would it be possible by looking at the sum of departmental plans or at the overall vision for the university to develop institutional academic priorities for the use of technology?

6. Does the plan include details of its cost of implementation? How precise or realistic do these costs appear? How much of the costs are for networks, hardware, and software, and how much for technical support staff, educational technology support staff, and educational applications? If there is funding for educational applications elsewhere in the strategic plan, what is the ratio of technology infrastructure investment to educational applications of the technology?

7. What steps could you take, if you were (or are) the academic president or vice president to ensure that academic priorities for the use of technology were well-defined and integrated into technology infrastructure planning? In your view, is this likely to lead to more or less spending on infrastructure in any one year?

8. When was the technology plan finalized or approved? Is this a rolling plan, updated every year? How will the plan be used?

9. You may want to go back to look at some of the technology plans available on the Web listed at the end of Chapter Two. What is the best plan you found? Why? What is the worst? Why?

The reason for asking these questions is that it is easy and not uncommon for the technology infrastructure to be built with no regard for the academic or educational requirements or priorities. Historically, information technology has tended to be introduced in higher education first to support administrative data processing requirements, such as student registration, financial management, office word processing, and internal communications. It is only recently (within the last five years) that academic requirements for technology support have become a central planning issue.

Also, because information technologies have such a variety of applications, certain infrastructure decisions can be made irrespective of the academic plans for using these technologies. For instance, there is a value in providing a networked computer for every academic, whether or not that professor is going to use it for teaching purposes. This will enable internal administrative communications to be more effective through e-mail. It may lead to savings in secretarial support if the faculty member learns how to do word processing. It will directly benefit the individual academic if he or she can contact research colleagues around the world through e-mail, set up individual Web pages to publicize research, and produce camera-ready copy for journal articles.

Consequently, there has been a tendency in many higher education institutions for educational requirements to be treated as of secondary importance to administrative requirements, an option or a nice-to-have, but not as essential for the day-to-day operation of the institution. The academic side has been slow or has found it difficult to define its technology needs and strategies clearly, or to agree on priorities, or to urge strongly that academic technology needs should be met.

The computers and communications support people have usually been able to identify more accurately the next level of technological development that is coming through. In comparison, the academic side has often been unable or unwilling to decide on priorities for the application of technology to teaching. So in order to meet ill-defined future academic needs, the technology people tend to ensure that the technological infrastructure is continually updated according to the highest possible technical standards, so that whatever academic requirements eventually become defined, the infrastructure is in a better position to meet these requirements. The most obvious example of this is the continual upgrading of desktop computers as they become faster and more powerful, independent of any identified applications or needs that can *only* be served by the more advanced machines.

For these reasons, it could be argued that it would be unwise to limit investments in technology infrastructure until clear academic priorities for its use have been defined. The availability of a new technology may open up possibilities for new applications that could not have been considered before the investment. Thus, one strategy for technology investment would be always to keep as close to the leading edge of developments as possible.

However, this can be a very expensive strategy, because what drives investment in technology in this scenario is the rapid change in technology and not the academic priorities of the institution. Without a clear academic strategy for the use of technology for teaching, senior managers are in no position to argue against the technology plan submitted by the head of computing and telecommunications services. This is particularly true if the institution as a whole understands the importance of technology but does not have a clearly defined academic strategy or set of academic priorities for its use.

Thus, the more an institution commits itself to the use of technology for teaching purposes, the more important it becomes to build academic applications and priorities into decisions and plans regarding technology infrastructure. In Chapter Two, one strategy suggested for achieving this is to require academic departments to develop their own teaching plans with the use of technology clearly identified in the plans. These plans can then be aggregated across an institution to identify key priorities for technology investment. However, it requires some central organization and coordination on the *academic* side to do this, probably somewhere in the academic vice president's office.

Key Issues in Technology Infrastructure

Technology infrastructure is, of course, as essential as the foundations of a house. Like the foundations of a house, it is often built first. However, although essential, technology infrastructure is not sufficient. Unfortunately, too often too much is spent on infrastructure (the foundations) so that there is little left for the rest of the house (the applications).

The infrastructure needs to be built so that it is compatible with and appropriate for the rest of the house (administrative needs, teaching needs, information management needs). Too often teaching needs are ill-defined compared with needs in the other areas, or when they are defined it is difficult to reach consensus on priorities.

Technology infrastructure is a big expenditure item. Because of the rapid rate of technological change, there is no sign that the expenditure will abate over the next few years. At the same time, the cost of investment should be set against the potential for revenue achieved by reaching out to new target groups and from sales of materials and services, and the likely academic benefits—that is, more cost-effective teaching and learning. However, the increase in costs can be predicted more confidently and measured more accurately than the increase in revenues and benefits.

Student Access to Technology

Nowhere is the need to identify academic priorities and strategies for the use of technology more important than in deciding on how to support student access to technology. An institution can construct the most sophisticated technology infrastructure to support teaching, but if students cannot access the technology all the investment is wasted.

Who Owns Computers?

Particularly for distance education students—but also for on-campus students—access to computer technology is a major issue. In 1998, 36 percent of households in Canada had at least one member who had direct Internet access from either work or home, and 23 percent of Canadian households had direct Internet access from home (Statistics Canada, 1998). Access among university students is higher. An IBM survey in 1998 found 60 percent of university and college students in the United States had convenient computer access. At UBC, 70 percent of all undergraduates have Internet accounts with the university. In Canada, Internet access costs an average of $13 a month (in U.S. dollars), in the United States $20 a month, and in Britain $44 a month (again in U.S. dollars).

However, although access continues to grow, it is strongly related to income, gender, and profession. Many of those who do have computers have machines that are not suitable for multimedia or Internet access. Student or family ownership of a computer is likely to vary considerably both between institutions and within institutions. Colleges with a mandate to serve disadvantaged groups are likely to find much lower access to computers among their target groups than institutions with high tuition fees and highly selective admission requirements. Even in one institution, engineering, computing, and business students will have higher computer ownership rates than liberal arts students. In liberal arts, socioeconomic status will affect student access; the higher the income levels at home, the more likely the ownership of a computer. Finally, computer ownership rates vary considerably not only between different countries but even in different geographical regions in the same country.

Socioeconomic patterns of computer ownership are significantly different from those for other domestic audiovisual equipment. Although the very poor for obvious reasons have had lower and later levels of ownership, and university professors have often been the last to jump on the domestic hardware bandwagon, low-income earners have traditionally been the early adopters of color televisions, laser discs, audiocassette players, compact disc players, and so on. This is not true, though, of personal computers; low-income families have preferred to buy video and computer games instead.

The rate and pattern of growth of personal ownership of computers is dynamic and changing rapidly. The proportion of homes in both the United States and Canada with a personal computer has increased faster over the last few years than it did with the adoption of any previous domestic entertainment equipment. Statistics Canada (1999) found that in 1998, Internet access from home increased 44 percent over the previous year. In Alberta, the province with the highest access, 45 percent of homes were connected. Statistics Canada also revealed that the proportion of women to men using the Internet went from 28 percent to 51 percent in one year (1998). Although teenage boys still spend the most time on-line, the second heaviest "surfers" when it comes to time spent on-line are seniors (people over sixty-five years of age).

In the last year or so, we have begun seeing whole cohorts of students coming into universities and colleges who have had access to computers since they started school. But many schools still do not have adequate computer provision, so students are entering university or college with widely different levels of computer literacy. In any case, ownership of a computer does not necessarily mean the student has the necessary computer skills for studying.

What all of the foregoing indicates is that we have to be very careful in the assumptions we make about computer ownership and use. One strategy would be to survey students (or potential students) about their current personal access to computers. The power of the machine, whether the student has Internet access, and ownership of peripherals such as a printer and CD-ROM drive, are also important data. Students should be asked not only what they have now but also what they are planning or willing to get.

However, there is also a chicken-and-egg issue here. If students are not required to have a computer for their studies, they are less likely to purchase one. If students who are thinking of purchasing a computer are not given clear specifications as to what is needed, they are more likely to purchase a less powerful model.

Nevertheless, it would be reasonable to assume that within five years, at least in North America, most students attending a research university, both on campus and off, will have their own computers and Internet access. The picture is not so clear for colleges and smaller universities. Certainly for colleges and universities with a mandate to serve students from low-income families, the assumptions about personal ownership of computers, and the suitability of campus infrastructures to support extensive computer-based learning, will be very different.

Computer Access Strategies

In other words, a single and systemwide university or college policy for student access to computers is probably unwise. The policy will need to vary from institution to institution, and even within the same institution there will need to be different policies in different areas. Still, every university or college will need to put in place a computer access policy, even if it is to make a deliberate choice that students will *not* need their own computers to study at a particular institution. The worst situation is where there is no policy and students find they need different computers for different courses or cannot access any facilities provided on campus because they are inadequate for the demand.

Several strategies can be used to provide support for student access to computers (see Resmer, Mingle, and Oblinger, 1995, for an excellent review).

One strategy is to provide computer labs on campus for students. Again, this is a useful start-up strategy, but in the long run it becomes unsustainable as the primary source of student support.

There are several drawbacks to relying on computer labs for access. The first is that as the use of computers for learning increases, capital costs get out of control. As well as finding money to add new machines as demand increases, institutions will have to find increasing amounts each year to replace existing machines, given the rate of technological change. If demand exceeds the availability of workstations, students have to book times or the time they have to wait becomes unacceptable. This removes one of the main advantages of using technology, its flexibility.

There will always be a need for specialized computer labs for those subject areas requiring exceptionally high-end or specialized machines and software. There will also always be a need for on-campus access through plug-in ports or drop-in labs for casual use. However, if a majority of students entering university or college already have their own computers and Internet access, in the long run the most flexible and cost-effective approach is to put in place policies that help and encourage those students without a computer and Internet access to provide their own.

Resmer, Mingle, and Oblinger (1995) suggest that the cost of universal access should be paid for jointly by students and the institution and that any financing plan should involve student "possession" of a computer and the use of technology fees. In my view, however, such a policy should not be implemented unless it is clear that students will need a computer, and that means ensuring there are sufficient courses designed to exploit fully the instructional benefits of using a computer. Will access to a computer be compulsory for certain courses? Will a whole program require computer access? Which courses or programs should be the first to implement such a policy? Will there be common technical standards for computers for all the courses in a program requiring the use of a computer?

Students will need answers to these questions. This requires each department to develop a clear strategy for the use (or deliberate non-use) of computers, and this strategy needs to be clearly communicated to potential students. The computer strategy should naturally emerge from the academic planning process in a department. These departmental strategies need to be coordinated at a faculty and institutional level so that students do not continually have to change machines, operating systems, Internet service providers, and so on.

In California, Sonoma State University spent two and a half years preparing for the implementation of a policy requiring all freshmen students to have computers. The university made sure that there were sufficient courses developed in a way that exploited the use of a computer and therefore made it essential and valuable to use one. This required a significant investment in faculty development.

Sonoma State also put in place a whole range of strategies to help students who could not afford computers. The institution introduced a work-on-campus scheme whereby students could get a computer and then work to pay it off. Relatively few students at Sonoma qualified for some form of supplementary state or federal grant that would enable them to purchase a computer, because those eligible for a grant were usually already "maxed out," that is, already receiving maximum allowable benefit. For these students, there was a low-cost rental scheme, and for some, free loans of computers from a pool donated by IBM and Apple.

Sonoma State found that there was very high compliance with its policy of requiring all freshmen students to have a computer. The policy was well received by parents and by employers, who praised the university for making higher education more relevant. Most students also seemed to be pleased with the policy. The important point here is that it was a total strategy. Implementing only part of it—such as a technology fee when many students clearly would not need to use a computer for their studies—can lead to considerable student and faculty resistance.

Some institutions have taken a somewhat different approach from Sonoma's to providing computer access for all students. The University of Minnesota at Crookston and two relatively small colleges in Canada—Acadia in Nova Scotia and Collège Boréal in Northern Ontario—have required every student to have an IBM ThinkPad laptop computer.

At UBC, the strategy we have adopted for the on-line courses we offered in conjunction with Monterrey Institute of Technology was different from Sonoma's and Collège Boréal's. First, because of the content area and target group, we assumed that all participants would already have access to a computer and the Internet. Also, because we wanted to reach participants on a global basis, we wanted a very simple standard: access to and ability to use Netscape 3.1 or later. However, this approach would not necessarily be appropriate for other content areas and target groups.

The real challenge for a department considering requiring students to have computer access is in ensuring that the computer will provide genuine value-added teaching. In other words, the computer will bring to the learning experience something unique and valuable to the student. Merely replicating lecture notes on the Web is not a good enough reason to require a student to find approximately $2,000 in addition to all the other costs he or she may have to carry as a college student.

The worst policy is to make computer access optional. This gives those students already with a computer an advantage over those who do not. It also marginalizes the technology application because if students can manage without a computer, why should they use one? Again, we are just increasing the work of both the teacher and the student without any clear, added benefit. Most important of all, this is a lazy policy because it relieves the department or the individual faculty member from having to think through a proper strategy for the use of computers for teaching.

My own preference is not to have institutionwide computer requirements for all students, especially at large institutions. Architecture and computer science are likely to have a much greater need for specialist software and high-end performance than English literature or philosophy. At the same time, there should be universitywide policy and planning, and good communication, so that if students move between subject areas they can make plans for computer purchase.

The role that the computer plays will vary depending on the teaching approach as well as the subject matter. For instance, in physiology, high-end stand-alone multimedia machines with high levels of student-machine interaction may be appropriate. In contrast, women's studies courses may require the cheapest possible machines (to increase access) but good discussion-forum software and powerful and widespread network access linking faculty to both on-campus students and community groups and individuals off campus.

Providing the hardware, software, and networks is just the tip of the iceberg. Learners must feel comfortable with the technology and know how to use it effectively. Because of variations in computer literacy levels, many universities and colleges are now providing courses and workshops to improve students' computer literacy. Many campus libraries combine instruction on using the Internet with library search strategies, and in the same way that many universities and colleges have established writing centers, so too some are now developing computer literacy drop-in centers.

Finally, although technology for the use of teaching is leading to the convergence of on-campus and off-campus teaching, there are still significant differences in student requirements between the two types of students. Applications that run over fast Ethernet or fiber-optic cable or on stand-alone fast machines in a computer lab will probably not run at all well over narrowband public telephone networks or on slow computers in the student's home. This has to be considered in the initial design of a course.

Role of Government in Widening Access

There is a strong role for government in widening access to the use of information technology for higher education, especially for disadvantaged groups. A number of states in the United States have developed their own private networks, such as Access Indiana, through contract leasing or bulk buying of telecommunications services. Through a "request for proposal" (RFP) process, government can invite submissions from providers to meet certain predefined standards, such as minimum service levels to all rural communities, high-speed links between universities and colleges, and flat-rate charges, based on volume rather than distance. Service providers then compete with one another to come up with a proposal that best meets the needs at the best price. However, this requires a relatively deregulated and genuinely competitive telecommunications environment, where government can lever its purchasing power between competing telecommunications companies.

In British Columbia, the provincial government has established a Provincial Learning Network that links all government offices, universities, hospitals, colleges, and schools. One of the key criteria for the award of the contract was that all rural schools would be provided with a minimum level of Internet and telecommunications services, at a flat-rate price based on volume, not distance.

Governments can also provide tax relief for students (or parents) on computer purchase. Lastly, government (either at a state or municipal level) can support the development of local community learning centers equipped with advanced technologies. These can provide open access to technology similar to a local library providing access to books. University and college lobbying can therefore influence government to facilitate access to learning technologies.

Although technology may open up access to some and deny it to others, the requirement for students to have their own computers would not be the main obstacle to university access in most North American research universities. Many more potential students are denied access by restrictive grade point average (GPA) entrance requirements, arbitrary prerequisites, residency or attendance requirements, and barriers to credit transfer from other institutions.

At UBC, the required grade point average for some faculties is higher than the level set for academic purposes because of the shortage of physical space (classrooms) and teachers. We shall see that the intelligent use of technology should enable modest increases in capacity that would enable admission GPAs to be more closely related to academic rather than space and personnel requirements. If a primary purpose of introducing technology-based learning is to increase access, then these admission policy issues need to be addressed as well.

Conclusions

Graves et al. (1997, p. 447) make the point that "information technology costs a lot today and will cost even more in the future. Institutions must plan to spend more money on IT if they are to maximize the benefits." Although technology infrastructure is important, it is not just a capital cost but also requires high operating costs, which brings it directly into competition for funds for teaching and research.

It is important that any increased expenditure strikes the appropriate balance between technology infrastructure, technical support, administrative applications, and educational applications. Some institutions that have already invested heavily in infrastructure and its technical support and administrative applications may need to spend less in these areas in the future and more on educational applications.

In addition, there should be strong links and integration between the overall technology plan and the use of technology for teaching and learning, and these in turn should be integrated with the overall vision and strategic directions of the institution. Although other applications of technology, such as administrative and financial systems, will remain important, teaching and learning requirements will demand increasing priority in an institution's technology plan. This means that an institution needs to put in place mechanisms for identifying academic needs and priorities and ensuring that they are taken into account in technology planning. This needs to push right down to the departmental and discipline level.

Finally, the issue of student access to technology is very sensitive. There is a tension between the students' need to use technology to improve the quality of their learning and issues of equity and universal access to higher education. Although the socioeconomic context of personal computer ownership is dynamic, in most institutions there will always be at least a minority who will not be able to afford their own computers and Internet access. Furthermore, there are wide variations both between and within institutions in students' prior ownership of computers, and therefore each institution is likely to have a different strategy for supporting student access to technology.

I have suggested that in the long run, as the use of computers for teaching and learning spreads throughout the institution, it will become economically unsustainable for a university or college to provide all the needed access on campus through specially provided computer labs. It will be better to assume that at least a majority of students will be able to provide their own computers and Internet access, and to focus help and support on those who most need it.

It is also essential that requirements for students to have access be dependent on a clearly articulated and defined teaching and learning role for computers, which will provide learners with educational opportunities that otherwise would not be available to them. If that test cannot be met, it is hard to justify the cost to the students or the institution. Thus, each academic department must have a clear academic rationale for the use of technology for teaching as well as policies in place that articulate both the computer requirements and the responsibility of the institution and the students in meeting those requirements. Finally, these policies need to be clearly communicated to students.

Chapter Five

Supporting Faculty

For many valid reasons, faculty members have a good deal of independence and autonomy. Furthermore, the way most universities and colleges are managed results in full-time tenure-track faculty having a major say in academic policies. This extends into setting criteria for appointment, tenure, and promotion of other faculty members through the peer review system. Mechanisms such as senate and peer review are fundamental to ensuring that tenure-track faculty set academic agendas, determine quality in content, and reward colleagues according to the standards laid down by faculty members themselves. This autonomy and power is considered necessary both to maintain academic freedom and to enable faculty members to create new knowledge through research and publication.

Research is by its nature unpredictable. Pure research in particular requires a high element of intellectual risk-taking and may not lead to immediate commercial benefits, although in the long term it may bring unknown and unforeseen economic advantage. Because of the high level of expertise and knowledge required to conduct research successfully, it is not surprising that determining priorities for research and creating opportunities to do it is one aspect of their work that faculty members jealously guard.

Because of the central role that faculty members play in the work of universities and colleges, any change, especially in core activities such as teaching and research, is completely dependent on their support. Presidents may dream visions, and vice presidents may design plans, and deans and department heads may try to implement them, but without the support of faculty members nothing will change.

Faculty members will change only if they can clearly see the benefits of change or the disadvantages of not changing. Any strategies for implementing the use of technology for teaching need to take into account the prevailing culture of the university, and above all that of the faculty members.

What Drives Faculty Behavior?

Finnegan (1997) suggests that over the last ten to twenty years, there has been a growing imbalance in supply and demand between tenure-track positions and those seeking tenure-track positions. The rapid expansion in the 1960s of universities and colleges led to a large increase in young, tenured faculty. The slowing down in the 1980s of growth in higher education institutions, and in particular the failure to fund new positions in proportion to the increases in student numbers, combined with an aging tenured professoriate, has resulted in far fewer tenure-track positions than qualified applicants. In practice, research universities in particular have levered this to obtain the best research candidates, with a result that research publication is now in many universities and colleges (whether or not research is in their mandate) the predominant or even the only criterion for appointment, tenure, and promotion.

One of the less obvious side effects of the emphasis on research publication for tenure and promotion is that many young instructors are unwilling to put in the effort required to develop technology-based teaching approaches, although they often have more familiarity with computer technology than their senior professors. They are advised instead to concentrate on research publications and the Ph.D. that is obligatory for most North American tenure track positions. The Ph.D., of course, is training for research, not teaching.

Because, at least in research universities, most faculty members are appointed—particularly with regard to tenure or tenure-track positions—primarily as a result of their research interests and record, few are exposed to any form of training in teaching. The learning mode with respect to picking up teaching skills reflects a craft-based or industrial model of apprenticeship, where new faculty follow the same approaches to teaching as their senior professors, who themselves had no training in teaching methods. Some recent graduates or postgraduates who become teaching assistants may receive some basic training from a faculty development office, but this is extremely brief and cursory compared with the preparation given, for example, to graduates wishing to become schoolteachers.

A more radical approach to balancing research with teaching was suggested in the Dearing Commission report on higher education in Britain (Dearing, 1997; also available at http:// www.leeds.ac.uk/educol/ncihe/natrep.htm). As a result of Dearing's recommendations, a national Institute for Teaching and Learning in Higher Education has been created in the United Kingdom. This aims to be a professional body for teachers in higher education. In order to become a member of the institute, university professors must demonstrate teaching proficiency. It is worth quoting verbatim the relevant sections in the Dearing report (http://wwwd2.leeds.ac.uk/ncihe/nr_123.htm):

§8.59. We believe that the necessary recognition of teaching in higher education will only be achieved through a national scheme of teacher accreditation to which all institutions voluntarily commit. . . . To cater for differing institutional perspectives and approaches to learning and teaching, we favour the recognition of institutional programmes leading to the accreditation of staff who have successfully completed a recognised programme.

§8.60. From the point of view of staff, a national scheme has the merit of providing a professional recognition with standing across the whole of higher education.

§8.61. While initial professional development will be the basis for establishing the professionalism of teaching, we consider it essential that staff should be encouraged to enhance and update their skills. To that end, we see advantage in establishing an organisation that can accredit training and practice, and recognise excellence in teaching at higher levels of recognised status. Such a body should have national standing, as in other professions. We propose the creation of an Institute for Learning and Teaching in Higher Education. To encourage teaching of the highest quality, the Institute would confer associate membership, membership, and fellowship to recognise superior levels of expertise.

§8.70. An important initial task for the Institute will be to assist the sector in making the best use of information technology.

Although this external encouragement or stimulus may lead to change, it is difficult to see how it can be immediately applied in the North American context. In the meantime, it will be left to provosts and academic vice presidents to do what they can to establish teacher-scholar models, such as Boyer's (1990), which can form the basis for evaluation of faculty for appointment, tenure and promotion.

Until then, though, what still drives faculty behavior in most universities, and even in many colleges, is the need to research and publish, and this in turn is driven by the close relationship between research publication and appointment, tenure, and promotion. In contrast, although many professors take their teaching very seriously, teaching in general is seen as a necessary evil, and one that should interfere as little as possible with research activities.

The problem is that teaching with technology is not something that can easily be picked up along the way, as something to be done off the side of the desk while engaged in more important or time-consuming activities such as research. It should be apparent by now that the use of technology for teaching and learning needs to be accompanied by some major changes in the way faculty members are trained and rewarded. I will deal with the training side first.

Faculty Training and Development

Green (1998), in a survey of campus information technology strategies, found that officials in his survey rated assisting faculty to integrate technology into instruction as the single most important information technology issue confronting their organization.

As a consequence, the American Productivity & Quality Center (APQC), in conjunction with the State Higher Education Executive Officers Association, conducted a benchmarking exercise on best practices in faculty instructional development in the use of technology in teaching (American Productivity & Quality Center, 1999). This involved the participation of forty-eight educational institutions and corporations from across the United States that came together to examine best practices in this area. As a result of a survey sent to seventy higher education institutions and several for-profit organizations selected by the forty-eight participant organizations, five educational institutions, one business corporation, and one government agency were chosen as best-practice "partners." Participants in the study visited each of the seven best-practice partners, and a report was prepared based on the site visits and the data returned by thirty-five of the higher education institutions and seven for-profit organizations that were surveyed. A range of criteria was used to select these institutions, but the overriding criterion was demonstrated excellence in the use of technology for teaching.

The selected best-practice institutions were Arthur Andersen Performance and Learning, Chicago; Bellevue Community College, Washington State; California State University Center for Distributed Learning, Rohnert Park; Collège Boréal, Sudbury, Ontario; University of Central Florida, Orlando; U.S. Air Force Air Command and Staff College, Montgomery, Alabama; and Virginia Tech, Blacksburg.

The findings from the final report of the APQC study were not entirely as expected. The first finding was that faculty development practice in an institution was strongly influenced by the institution's overall approach to the use of technology for teaching. Faculty development seemed to work best when the institution had a culture pervaded by the use of technology and supported by a wide range of strategies, including the following:

- A strong strategic plan in which the use of technology for teaching played a prominent role
- Extensive investment in technology infrastructure
- Support from senior leadership for the use of technology for teaching
- Support, in a wide variety of ways, for faculty members who wished to use technology for teaching
- Support for students through computer access, Internet accounts, and financial support

The report concluded that although these approaches individually can create a positive atmosphere for faculty instructional development, their *combination* appears to result in a culture that is "totally immersed" in teaching and learning with technology. This suggests that depending on faculty development as the main strategy for technological change may not be sufficient in itself.

Another finding was that best-practice organizations focused on teaching and learning, not on technology itself, in faculty development. However, often they had to deal with faculty computer literacy before they could move on to educational or instructional issues.

Virginia Tech has managed to get 96 percent of all faculty to go through a faculty development program and 50 percent of all faculty by 1999 have gone through a second faculty development program. This is expected to increase to 75 percent in the next year or so.

Virginia Tech has done this by linking the provision of a modern desktop computer to participation in a faculty development program. In order to get a new computer, faculty had to agree to participate in a short training course on using the computer for teaching. Since computers are replaced every four years, faculty training becomes a recurrent cycle.

Virginia Tech has found a way to introduce faculty members gradually to concepts of instructional design by recognizing the prevailing institutional culture, and in particular the context in which faculty members are working. In the words of John Moore, director of educational technologies, "The notion of instructional design is eased in. It is not laid on with a shovel."

The Faculty Development Institute at Virginia Tech uses a problem-based approach to training. The faculty members work in small groups with an instructor in preparing a lesson using relatively simple approaches to the use of computer technology, such as making a set of Web pages for a network-based course. This not only enables the basic operation of the computer to be covered but also allows teaching issues to surface and be dealt with, at which point basic issues of instructional design can be raised. One reason for the relatively high return rate for the second round of development programs is the interest in the process of teaching generated by the initial training programs.

Another critical factor in the success of this faculty development program was the leadership provided by the vice president of information systems and the provost, who reallocated substantial funds from a state equipment trust fund to support the faculty development activity. The program also had support from the deans, ensuring that faculty members were released from some teaching duties to attend the faculty development program.

A somewhat related faculty development issue was identified at each of the five higher education best-practice institutions in the APQC benchmarking study. Although managers usually consider instructional, graphic, and interface design to be essential to the development of high-quality learning materials, faculty members tend to oppose or avoid direct instruction in these areas. Design concepts need to "emerge" in response to dealing with real teaching issues rather than be taught directly to faculty members. Consequently, faculty development initiatives at the APQC best-practice institutions were often oriented to particular issues or projects with respect to the teaching of the subject.

All this comes back to the project management model (discussed in Chapter Three). Several of the best-practice institutions in the APQC study found that faculty members started to rethink the teaching and learning process through the process of creating instructional software in a project team. For instance, the Center for Distributed Learning for the California State University system uses a well-defined Development Process Map, which emphasizes hands-on, problem-solving contexts, not what technology can do (http://cdl.edu). Thus, faculty development in instructional design and the use of technology occurs best in a context of tackling a specific teaching and learning problem.

The importance of project management relates to another interesting finding from the study. A "screening" survey of thirty-five higher education institutions was used to select best-practice partners. Twenty-six (65 percent) of the screening respondents stated that the team approach was the most effective strategy for developing technology-based courses, but only five (12 percent) of those surveyed actually used a team approach. This contrasts with the seven best-practice partners in the APQC study, all of whom used a team approach. It is clear that one important goal for faculty development is to prepare instructors for teamwork and to locate faculty development in a project team context.

In the study, faculty development for using technologies for teaching was both a centralized and a decentralized activity. Most best-practice institutions had at least one institutionwide center to support faculty development, and many also had a separate center for distributed learning. However, most best-practice institutions also drew heavily on other organizational units to support faculty development initiatives in technology-based learning. Collaboration among different units was essential, and some institutions had created positions or allocated responsibilities for the coordination not just of faculty development but of general instructional support for faculty.

Relying just on a central faculty development office for faculty training in the use of technology for teaching was often a problem. Although expert in teaching and learning generally, staff in the faculty development office often lacked specific expertise or skills in using technologies for teaching or were even philosophically antagonistic to the idea.

Another finding was less surprising: faculty members learn best from their peers through show-and-tell demonstrations by faculty "stars" who have developed good examples of technology-based teaching. The report recommended that faculty development offices need to track instructors who develop high-level skills in using technology and make use of them in faculty development initiatives.

The University of Central Florida uses "Web Vets"—faculty members who have completed teaching on-line courses—as mentors for first-time on-line instructors. Collège Boréal trains young faculty members in both technical and instructional skills, then assigns them to each college to serve as "coaches" or mentors for other faculty members. (See the following section on alternative support strategies for more on Collège Boréal.)

Overall, these strategies have been extremely successful, leading to widespread adoption of technology-based teaching in all the best-practice institutions in the APQC study. In contrast, the most common form of training given to instructors in most institutions is to show those interested in using technology for teaching how to use the technology. This, though, is starting at the wrong place.

Many instructors need to understand *why* it is important to use technology for teaching in the first place, and for what purposes. In particular, training should be related to the changing environment in which universities find themselves and the changing needs of learners. Second, some basic understanding of the teaching and learning process, and in particular the different kinds of teaching approaches and the goals they are meant to achieve, need to be understood. New technologies need to be related to these different teaching approaches. Third, instructors need to understand the different roles that technology can play in teaching, and how this alters the way that teaching needs to be organized. Only then does it make much sense to train faculty in how to use a particular piece of technology, and even then it may be better *not* to teach them the technical details of using technology but leave that to other specialists in the team.

However, although this sequence may be logical and would provide the most thorough preparation for instructors wishing to use technology for teaching, it is unlikely to be the most pragmatic way, given the prevailing campus culture. In reality, it would take a good deal of time to go through the professional training required to build a teaching approach based on modern theories of teaching and learning and linked to differences in technology (although such courses do exist on-line: see http://itesm.cstudies.ubc.ca/info). Many faculty members would see this approach as unnecessarily time consuming and be concerned that it would further delay or interfere with their research activities, which they need for tenure or promotion.

For most faculty members, then, faculty development should not be treated as a separate, independent activity but be embedded in a broad range of strategies that support technology-based teaching and learning. It should be available as far as possible on a just-in-time basis and be integrated within a project team approach.

Dealing with the Professor's Fear of the Computer

Although professional development opportunities for instructors are essential, they are not sufficient to ensure support for and adoption of technology for teaching. Indeed, framing the issue as one of training faculty can actually be counterproductive because it tends to put the "blame" on faculty members. "Faculty are the problem; we have to fix them. Training is the answer." This is framing the issue incorrectly. Training or professional development really is the last stage in a broader change process.

In any institution, different faculty members will be in different positions along the change process, which runs the gamut from fear to anger, resistance, grieving for the old, cautious adoption of innovation, and finally total belief in or championing of the change. Strategies need to be developed to address each one of these steps toward change.

Fear is perhaps the biggest obstacle to change, and it leads directly to anger targeted at changes that feed the fear. It is important for managers advocating change to recognize that faculty members *do* have some justifiable fears and to strive to remove the justification.

The biggest fear is likely to be loss of tenure or replacement by a machine. One simple—perhaps too simple—strategy to deal with that is to announce that there will be no redundancies due to technological change. This is also likely to be an announcement that a president may live to regret. A more constructive strategy is to communicate on a regular basis with the faculty association or whatever organization represents instructors in pay and bargaining negotiations. The aim is to show why the strategy of moving to greater use of technology for teaching and learning would benefit both instructors and learners. Another aim is to seek the faculty association's support in the use of technology for improving the quality of the institution's teaching, and thus help to secure the long-term future of the institution.

The whole issue of appointment, tenure, and promotion needs to be reviewed, for the reasons set out by Finnegan (1997). One factor that will assist this process is the rapid aging of the professoriate in North America. In many institutions, 40 percent to 60 percent of faculty will retire within five years. This will ease to some extent the competitive pressure for tenure-track positions and allow for a wider range of criteria for promotion to be introduced, including innovative and effective uses of technology for teaching, instead of the sole criterion of research publications.

However, some institutions will not want to wait another five years before introducing new technologies. This will mean a systematic review of the appointment, tenure, and promotion process department by department. Again, this will work only if faculty members see that this is in their best interest. Many prefer to research rather than teach; for those who teach, personal interaction with, and knowledge of, individual students is often the most rewarding aspect. Some fear that technology will reduce that per-

sonal contact. This fear needs to be addressed by providing a balanced approach to the use of technology and face-to-face teaching, especially on campus, and by pointing out that the intelligent
use of technology can lead to increased teacher-student interaction (as we saw in the Virginia Tech Math Emporium example described in Chapter One). For distributed learning and distance
education, the value of networking and student discussion forums,
which encourage interaction between instructor and learners,
needs to be stressed.

Another fear is that the use of technology will mean more work
for faculty members, or rather, will mean that faculty members will
have to spend more time on teaching and less on research. Under
current conditions in most universities and colleges, this a well-
grounded and justifiable fear. The Lone Ranger model, discussed
in Chapter Three, certainly increases the faculty workload, particularly if technology is used merely as an add-on to other existing
activities such as classroom teaching. A project management model
provides a means by which workload can be anticipated, shared,
and controlled.

The important point here is that there are legitimate fears arising from teaching by technology, and these fears need to be addressed in a constructive and open manner.

Alternative Support Strategies for Faculty

My institution, UBC, may be different from most, but I am seeing less and less resistance from faculty to the concept of using
technology—at least selectively—for teaching. I am seeing
though—throughout North America, Australia, and the United
Kingdom—increasing frustration from faculty at the lack of support they are getting from the institution. Training them to use the
technology will not help; indeed, it will merely exacerbate the situation, creating more demands for support that the institution
cannot meet.

The answer is to provide comprehensive and systematic technical and professional support for faculty. Although the project
management model may be the best way to support faculty, not all
technology-based teaching and learning can or should be forced
into that model. Technology is often used as a classroom aid, and

in addition, the Lone Ranger approach is still valid for small projects or for creating small technology-based modules, such as a Web site, to support classroom-based teaching. Instructors require assistance for such projects as well.

Collège Boréal has put in an interesting faculty support system. It has taken young faculty members, trained them in the use of technology for teaching, and allocated them at a ratio of one support person for every twenty faculty members on average (*all* instructors use technology for teaching at Collège Boréal). The support staff report to a central educational technology unit called La Cuisine but are delegated to work in a particular disciplinary area.

The college has no classes between 8:00 A.M. and 11:00 A.M. on Thursdays so faculty can work with their support staff on the design of their teaching. The support staff are trained not only in educational design and the use of technology but also in how to fix technical problems. When teaching, instructors can call on their support staff through a beeper system, so even simple problems such as the failure of a projector can be immediately resolved. After one or two years, support staff return to their regular teaching but are now fully expert in the use of new technologies.

In addition to the staff allocated to work with individual instructors, there are in La Cuisine several specialist staff members, such as multimedia designers and experienced instructional designers, who not only provide the training for support staff but also work on larger projects and provide advice and help to support staff.

Technology and instructional design support is the straw that may break the back of institutions that really want to use technology for teaching in a major way. If professors are not to be totally overloaded in the preparation of technology-based materials, and if technology is to be used well and reliably for teaching, then the support will need to be in the range of one technical support person to every twenty to thirty full-time instructors using technology. Furthermore, these support staff members need to be located close to the department (although they may work and report to a central unit). In addition, there needs to be at least one instructional design person–project manager for every thirty to fifty instructors. "Local" support staff will also need more specialized staff, such as graphics designers and interface designers, to draw on from more centralized units.

Thus, the primary costs of technology-based teaching will be in the support staff needed. If these support costs are not met, then instructors will either become hostile to technology-based teaching or other areas of their work, especially research, will suffer. Furthermore, such support staff needs to be integrated as much as possible into project teams.

Intellectual Property, Copyright, and Revenue Generation

Another way to reward faculty is to ensure that revenues generated by the use of technology in a department flow back into that department and do not get swallowed by the central bureaucracy. Innovative mechanisms need to be developed for instructors (and other creative staff) to share in rights and royalties from the development of generic educational software and learning materials.

Establishing Ground Rules

Nowhere is there more confusion, misinformation, and paranoia than in discussions of intellectual property and copyright surrounding the development and use of digital materials. I must warn you that I am not a lawyer, and the current law in most countries surrounding copyright and educational use is at best vague or untested with regard to educational digital materials. Nevertheless, I am convinced that instructors and students are consistently breaking copyright law, especially in their use of the Web, on a wide scale every day.

There is a lack of case law about educational use of digital copyrighted materials, partly because the stakes are so low, regarding the money involved in any breach of a particular copyright infringement. Copyright holders are reluctant to go to court over a relatively small amount of unpaid rights, although cumulatively the sums involved may be substantial. Furthermore, because of the widespread implications of a particular court challenge, it is likely that any case would go through several appeals all the way to the Supreme Court, resulting in huge litigation costs. Because no institution or organization wants to be the first to test the law, lawyers tend to be very cautious in their interpretation of the law.

Copyright laws originated in the sixteenth century, mainly to protect writers and producers of entertainment. By the mid-twentieth century they had been adapted mainly to serve large commercial interests, which needed copyright protection to cover their investment in the production of print materials, music, and performance.

These copyright laws, despite recent changes, do not adequately relate to the changing world of information technology. There is an urgent need to reform copyright law but an understandable reluctance to do this since the implications of new digital technologies for copyright law are by no means clear. The law is also not created as a result of a simple, logical analysis of the "facts." There are conflicting interests between creators and users of copyrighted material and, hence, intense lobbying to shape the law to protect or further different interests.

Nevertheless, in my experience, at least 90 percent of all cases involving digital teaching materials are adequately covered by existing law, so although there is an area of untested confusion due to new technologies in most cases the existing law is reasonably clear. Furthermore, distance educators have for over thirty years been dealing with the issue of copyright and intellectual property, with very few problems with either the courts or the producers of educational materials. Nevertheless, this experience and knowledge is continually ignored by academics and administrators coming new to the digital world of multimedia and the Web and wanting to rewrite copyright history.

Creating Copyrighted Material

It will help to clarify the difference, as I see it, between intellectual property and copyright. The law states that the creator of original material automatically owns the rights to that material. One does not have to register it. However, it must be something concrete, such as a book, a play, written or performed music, or a Web site. An idea or a thought does not have copyright protection because of the difficulty in law in proving where an idea originated. "Ideas" only have protection if there is a physical or tangible embodiment of them.

Whether or not it holds up legally, the distinction between intellectual property, defined as the original ideas and thoughts of an academic or teacher, and copyright of concrete materials, is a useful one. When my unit makes an agreement to develop a distance learning course, the university owns the rights to the materials created, but the academic is free to take the ideas and use them in other forms, such as a book or published article. Another set of laws, around conflict of interest, prevents an academic paid a regular salary by the university from developing similar materials for another organization without the university's permission.

These principles can easily be extended to the creation of digital educational materials provided that the institution puts in place a set of clear, written, advance agreements between the institution and the creators of the materials, a point I will return to shortly.

It will be helpful also to distinguish between the rights of teachers and learners and the rights of creators of educational materials. Up to now, universities and colleges have generally been heavily on the side of users of copyrighted material, that is, the teachers and learners. In particular, university and college librarians have lobbied heavily for liberal and unrestricted access to copyrighted materials for educational users. This is partly because institutions themselves have not generally been the creators of such materials. Publishers fund the production and marketing of books, and royalties go to the author.

The legal position of an academic employed full time by a university but writing a book for a publisher is an interesting one, especially if material in the book is a consequence of her regular work—for instance, research funded by or through the university. It could be argued that as an employee of the university, any material developed as a result of the full-time employment of an academic is legally the property of the employer, that is, the university or college. Universities and colleges have generally been happy to allow faculty members to publish independently because it is seen as work outside of or in addition to their regular teaching or research. Universities also recognize the importance of independent publishing as a means of disseminating and making public new knowledge as part of their public service obligation. However, with the increased development of digital materials *as part of the regular process of teaching,* universities and colleges are now themselves funding the creation of materials and becoming major stakeholders in and *producers* of copyrighted materials.

Why, though, would the individual teacher, the faculty member, not have the rights to digital materials published for courses, rather than the university? First, the academic is in a contractual relationship with the university. In short, he or she is paid to teach, research, and do some administration. If digital materials are created as part of that academic's regular work, in most countries the courts would support the view that the material belongs to the employer.

Second, digital material is increasingly being created not just by a single academic working in isolation but by a team of people. The academic may have an idea on how to use digital technology to create learning materials, but often it will require the skills and expertise of an instructional designer, an interface designer, a graphic artist, and a computer programmer to bring the idea to fruition. Indeed, most of the original thinking may come from the other members of the team if the content has already been well established in the field.

Third, the university or college is providing substantial funding, usually in the form of public funds, to enable the creation of this material. A CD-ROM, for instance, may cost more than $100,000 to develop without taking into account the time of the academic, which is also paid for by the university or college. The institution has a right to ensure that the materials created are available as widely as possible for learning purposes in the institution, and if possible, the institution has a duty to protect such public investment. I will return to how the academic contribution can be fairly rewarded without the university giving away the rights to the individual faculty member.

Fourth, the distinction between copyright and patents is also useful. Patent policy tends to be used for inventions or the conversion of research into commercial products. Many universities have patent policies in place that ensure that any revenues generated from inventions developed at the university with public funds are shared on a fair and agreed-upon basis between the research team, the academic department where the research team is based, and the university. A university patent policy can be used to distinguish between the creation of specific teaching material and the creation of generic digital tools that support the creation of other learning materials.

For instance, in developing teaching materials that require experimentation, a team may develop software that simulates laboratory experiments—a virtual lab. There will be two separate aspects of the teaching material: the simulation software and the content that is "dropped into" the simulation. The content may be specific to the subject area, but the simulation software, such as a virtual microscope or test analysis, could be used for a variety of topics or subject areas. In this case, the university would own the rights to the specific teaching material if it was created as part of the normal process of teaching. In contrast, the generic simulation software would be patented, and any revenues from sales would be shared among the developers (including the academic), the department, and the university in general.

WebCT is a good example of "generic" software, which is used in over six hundred universities and colleges and is now patented. CS315, An Introduction to Operating Systems, was the original course for which WebCT was developed, and the university owns the rights to the on-line course.

Underlying all this discussion is the issue of fairness. One has to be fair to producers of copyrighted material, especially if the creation of material required heavy investment and originality. Also, although one can hide behind the law, good employers should operate in a fair and reasonable manner. Thus, a balance needs to be found between the interests of its employees (of all kinds), its learners, and the public who provides the funding. I will come back to this when I have finished examining how copyright law actually works with respect to educational materials.

Using Copyrighted Material

The greatest confusion tends to arise from the use of third-party copyrighted material, that is, material created by someone else that is incorporated into otherwise original material. The most obvious example of this is a quotation from another work that is included in an article or book. It also applies to illustrations and graphics, and with digital materials, to sound and video clips.

Copyright law varies from country to country, although there is an international convention on copyright that many countries have signed and try to enforce regarding the use of materials copyrighted in another country. Some countries have special codicils or laws covering educational users; others make no distinction between educational and other users. Holders of large amounts of copyrighted material, such as publishers, may give permission and also charge for doing so, depending on whether the organization wanting to use copyrighted material is a for-profit or a nonprofit organization.

In most countries there is a "fair use" or "fair dealing" clause in the copyright bill, which allows for a small proportion of a work to be used without the need to seek permission from the copyright holder. This is one area where the law is very much open to interpretation, but a quotation of less than forty words from a prose work, or a couple of lines or less from a poem, is generally deemed "fair use" for educational purposes. In a classroom context in Canada and the United States, a lecturer may be allowed to reproduce a small proportion of illustrations from a book for lecture purposes and students may be able to make one copy of an article for personal use.

These practices have been established for traditional print media and they do not necessarily apply to digital material or even television or film. However, in the absence of explicit case law, it would be reasonable to assume that the courts would be sympathetic to the same principles of fair use for digital material.

Also, in some countries, universities and colleges have worked with major copyright holders to create a simple, "blanket" procedure for copyright clearance through a third-party agency, such as Cancopy in Canada. Getting permission from the original copyright holder can be a lengthy and time-consuming process. The administrative costs of obtaining and giving a copyright permission may be many times higher than the actual charge for use made by the copyright holder. Consequently, having a simple procedure offers advantages to both the users and the owners of copyrighted material. (There are also disadvantages with copyright collectives. Whereas a copyright holder may sometimes grant permission for educational use at no cost, copyright collectives will always charge a licensing fee.)

Requests for copyright clearance for the reproduction of an article for a stated number of copies for educational use can be sent to Cancopy, which charges a set rate based on the number of copies and the length or amount of material to be used. The maximum that can be reproduced under the Cancopy agreement is 20 percent of the original work. Cancopy collects the fee from the users and passes on the revenues to the copyright holders. This enables copyright to be cleared for a small amount, often within two weeks of the request being submitted. However, the Cancopy arrangement does not at the time of this writing cover digital materials.

Anyone wishing to incorporate third-party digital materials into his or her own materials, whether from a CD-ROM or from a Web site, should seek permission first unless it is covered by fair use or unless permission to copy materials is given in advance or as part of the purchase contract, such as clip-art from a CD-ROM. This permission, once given, may be for nonprofit or educational purposes only.

A common misconception is that an open Web site, that is, one not protected by a password, is copyright-free. This is not so. The creator of the Web site owns the copyright (the law does not specify a particular medium), and if you download the Web site to your own or another server, or make a printed copy of the site without permission, you are in breach of copyright. (If you think about it, the principle is exactly the same as for a library book. It may be publicly available and borrowed without charge, but the copyright still belongs to the publisher and it would be illegal to copy the book without permission.) Similarly, it is illegal to scan printed material into a Web site without permission from the copyright holder unless it is in the public domain (that is, the rights have expired, or the original copyright holder has waived all rights).

Unfortunately, getting permission to incorporate third-party materials into a Web site is often very difficult or impossible. Copyright is usually given conditionally, and in particular for a set number of users. Copyright holders are often rightly concerned that once their material is on the Web, they will lose all control over its use. Even where they are willing to give permission, it may take months to nail this down, and one of the features of the Web for educational purposes is its immediacy and speed.

Consequently, copyright law is being broken daily by individual academics copying other materials into their own Web sites or CD-ROMs without obtaining permission or paying the necessary fees. Just because it is for educational use does not remove the obligation to obtain permission, unless it is considered fair use or dealing. There is no case law for fair use or dealing for Web or CD-ROM materials. Therefore, it would be very risky to assume that copying a whole screen or illustration from a Web site or CD-ROM will be considered fair use or dealing by the courts, especially if it constitutes a major part of the work.

There is still one further twist on copyright. Very often copyright holders will provide free use, or use at moderate cost, for educational users, on the assumption that this will not be for commercial purposes. Increasingly, though, universities and colleges are trying to generate revenues or make profits from the production of multimedia and Web material. It is important that the actual use complies with the terms of the permission.

Advice on Copyright for Creators of Digital Materials

1. First, wherever possible, apply the same rules (if you know them) for print materials to the use of the Web; be cautious rather than take risks in interpreting these rules.
2. If in doubt, ask for permission. Many creators of Web sites with very useful digital materials, such as public museums and art galleries, have procedures in place for giving permission quickly and easily, and often without charge. Often all that is required is an e-mail. Information on copyright and permission is often available on Web sites.
3. Always password-protect your course site and provide access only to registered students and other known users, such as tutors. This allows you to specify accurately the number of likely users and makes copyright permission easier and cheaper to get. It also ensures privacy for the students.
4. Provide required printed readings in print format because it is easier to obtain permission.
5. Provide the url for another site as a hotlink, rather than copy and download information from that site.
6. Even if referring students to another site via a url, ask permis-

sion if the reading or exploration of the site requires students to spend a good deal of time at the site because this might not be deemed "fair use." (Think of it the other way round. How would you feel if someone else registered students in their institution and directed them to study your course or your research, without permission or acknowledgment?) This is one area where courts have stepped in and protected the rights of the creator of the original site.

7. Provide a rights statement on your own home site, stating that the site is copyrighted and materials cannot be copied or downloaded without permission. This will protect third-party material incorporated in the site as well as your own. Alternatively, provide a statement that the site is copyrighted and users are free to copy or download for noncommercial purposes, except (where appropriate) for certain parts of the site, which belong to third parties, thus again allowing you to protect third-party rights.

8. Always acknowledge the use of other material, even when permission is given to use it.

9. Do not give permission to other parties to use third-party material incorporated into your site; direct them to the third party or clear the permission from the third party yourself.

10. If your institution does not have a specialist or an administrative capacity to deal with copyright issues, establish one immediately. This problem is not going to go away. It is not a good use of academic time for a faculty member to spend hours or days negotiating copyright permissions and paying fees. Specialists do it more quickly and cheaply. The bookstore, the library, or a multimedia or distributed learning center are all possible places to locate this function, but ensure that it is adequately resourced to deal with copyright issues. Also, make sure that the person responsible for copyright policy is someone with common sense; an overly rigid interpretation of the law will quickly bring all educational media production to a halt.

11. Educate *all* your instructors, including nonpermanent staff. It is likely that the institution, not the individual, will be held responsible if you have not taken steps to inform instructors fully on the law and their obligations.

12. Finally, use project management to ensure that copyright issues are understood and ownership of materials are agreed by all parties, including the content experts. This can be done by drawing up a formal letter of agreement that includes a statement on copyright use *before* starting on course or Web site development (go to http://det.cstudies.ubc.ca/devman/ to see a sample letter of agreement).

Implications of Digital Copyright for Institutions

Moving to technology-based teaching has several major policy and rights implications for universities and colleges, particularly when the institution is investing large sums of money in the development of digital teaching and learning materials. Such a move will affect the relationship between academics, the institution, and publishers.

The first step is to establish clear rules and procedures regarding ownership of digital materials created in the course of teaching and research. Traditionally, academics have been free to negotiate independently with publishers their rights and royalties for books. The arrangement is that the publisher becomes the copyright holder and pays the author a royalty or percentage of revenues based on sales. I see no reason why this arrangement should be changed, even for digital materials, where an academic or subject expert is contracted by a publisher to provide expertise for a commercially produced CD-ROM or Web site.

There is a more curious arrangement for academic journal articles. As a condition of publication, the journal publisher usually requires the academic give the publisher the rights to the article, free of charge. Academic usually agree to this because of the importance of publication in refereed journals for appointment, tenure, and promotion. It is nevertheless a curious arrangement, because it means that access to papers based on often publicly funded research has become privatized and needs to be bought back at great expense by libraries through journal subscriptions, for use by future students. There is a lesson here for university- or college-created digital materials.

Universities and colleges, and even individual instructors, are beginning to negotiate with publishers for the commercial exploitation of extremely expensive digital learning materials created through university or college funding. However, in this case, a royalty arrangement, whereby the publisher obtains the rights in return for payment of royalties either to the academic or to the university or college, is a poor commercial deal for the educational institution.

All the front-end production costs have been borne by the institution, whereas in book publication, most of the production (and marketing) costs are borne by the publisher. For digital materials, the proportion of the costs devoted to marketing and distribution (although substantial) compared with production costs is likely to be far lower than for printed books. Universities and colleges should be careful that they do not give away too cheaply the rights for such materials. It is a cause for some concern that individual instructors, who may have contributed only a proportion of the work, should be allowed to negotiate with publishers as if they owned the rights to the materials. The ideal arrangement with a publisher would be to bring them into the project from the beginning, with a clear agreement about revenue sharing based on the relative costs to all parties in development and distribution.

The second issue is that institutions moving into revenue-generating or profit-making activities from the use of digital materials should be very careful to check that copyright permission covers such activities.

Rewarding Creators of Technology-Based Teaching and Learning Materials

Finally, how may not just faculty members but all the people involved in the production of digital learning materials that produce revenues for the institution be rewarded fairly if the institution retains the rights? I will try to answer that question now.

An institution can deal with this issue in several ways. Underlying my approach is a basic matter of principle. I believe that technology-based teaching should be a core part of the regular work of a faculty member as well as of the support staff who help develop the materials. Following this principle, a faculty member should get paid no more and no less for developing technology-based teaching than for classroom teaching. There are obvious dangers in developing two categories of teachers—those who use technology and get paid more (or less) and those who don't—no matter the quality of the teaching. Reward should be based on the overall quality and contribution to teaching, whether this is done through distributed learning or face-to-face teaching.

However, the development of technology-based learning materials and teaching through technology should be factored into the regular workload of faculty and staff support. In other words, it should replace something. The main problem facing faculty members working on technology-based teaching today is that far too often this is treated as ancillary or extra work on top of what they already do.

At UBC, we used to pay individual faculty members a personal honorarium for developing distance education materials. At least that way they got extra money for extra work. However, this just put more pressure on them. Many faculty members rightly believe that they now do not have adequate time to do teaching, research, or administration properly because they are being asked to do more and more. I changed the arrangement of paying the faculty member an honorarium (which merely covered the cost of a part-time sessional teacher and usually did not reflect the true cost of an experienced and senior academic) to transferring the same amount of money to the department. It is then negotiated between the head of department and the faculty member doing the work how best to use that money.

There are several advantages to this new arrangement. First, if the instructor is young and needs the money, the work can still be paid to cover extra load. Usually, however, what faculty members want is to be bought out from regular face-to-face teaching to have time to develop good quality materials. They also want good technical and educational support, which can cut down on their workload. Sometimes they cannot be released from face-to-face teaching, so the money is paid into a research fund to be used later when the technology project is finished. Also, because we pay the money to the department, we are covered if the professor leaves or goes on sabbatical; it is then a departmental responsibility to find a suitable replacement. And last, the head of department has some flexibility in assigning teaching requirements across both face-to-face and technology-based distributed learning.

Quality of teaching, no matter the format, needs to be a major criterion for appointment, tenure, and promotion. Successful innovation in teaching resulting in more cost-effective teaching and learning in particular needs to be rewarded. This means putting in place systematic and fair methods of teaching assessment. This need not be imposed from outside. It can be based on a professional process of peer review. The English and Scottish higher education funding councils have established rigorous procedures for assessing the quality of teaching in higher education based on internal peer review that have been well received by the British universities. This is an issue wider than just the use of technology for teaching, but without an internal process for assessing quality in teaching tied to tenure and promotion, there will be little encouragement for faculty to be innovative.

This comes back to a point made in Chapter One. Large investment in technology-based teaching can be justified only if it leads to significant changes in the ways we teach. In particular, that means replacing some of the things that are done now, such as large-size lectures, with technology-based learning, or using technology to generate substantially more revenues by reaching new target groups. Doing this will enable the costs of the additional work of developing technology-based learning to be fully covered or justified. Only by these radical changes in the way we organize and structure teaching and learning can faculty workload be kept down.

This means that the very sensitive issue of faculty agreements needs to be addressed. There are short-term advantages in leaving things loose, but technological innovation will become unsustainable as instructors become more experienced, suffer from increased workloads, and find that they are still unrewarded. Fortunately, many of the necessary measures are in the hands of faculty members themselves. As more and more academics become familiar with using technology for teaching and the demands that doing so places on them, they should become more willing to look at alternative arrangements for rewarding or encouraging innovation. This is a very good reason why the institutional administration should work closely with the faculty association or union on these issues.

Finally, money talks. Any profits or revenues generated externally through the development of technology-based teaching should return to the department and discipline groups that developed and delivered the program or courses. There is one caveat, though. Direct costs should be repaid first to all units, both academic and support, involved in production and delivery. This makes sure that those that actually do the work have their costs fully covered. At UBC, the deans have agreed to a split on revenues generated by distance education courses; a similar arrangement could be made for multimedia materials or Web courses. First, all direct costs are repaid, including overheads at a notional 25 percent, to both the department and the support units. Any surplus revenues then are split 75 percent to the department and 25 percent to the support units. The 25 percent to support units is to provide funds to support other new initiatives. The department can decide how to use the money returned.

There are other ways in which faculty and support units can be rewarded for or encouraged to use technology-based teaching and learning, but every institution wanting to move in this direction needs to think carefully about what will motivate its faculty members in particular to support such a move.

Conclusions

Faculty autonomy and independence are unique features of Western higher education systems. Indeed, they are core elements of what makes universities and colleges what they are.

Finnegan (1997) points to the danger of focusing too narrowly on the single criterion of research publications for tenure and promotion. This is leading to external demands for far greater accountability of universities and colleges, especially regarding teaching. The failure to give sufficient attention to teaching is actually leading to a gradual erosion of faculty autonomy, as government and employers exert increasing pressure on institutions through the introduction of measures of accountability.

One means of ultimately protecting faculty autonomy is to widen the criteria for appointment, tenure, and promotion to give greater emphasis to teaching ability and make sure that such criteria are really used when appointments, tenure, or promotion decisions are made. The recognition of the importance of this by faculty will also lead to their acceptance of the need for a more professional approach to teaching, which in turn will make training in the use of technology more acceptable.

Still, training must take into account faculty resistance to theoretical or time-consuming approaches to developing teaching skills. Strategies to avoid this include just-in-time problem-solving approaches to teaching, training by peers, time freed up from teaching or administration for formal professional development, and rewards for improved teaching performance, which may include grants or sabbatical awards, royalties to the department from sale of materials, and tenure and promotion.

Training alone though is unlikely to be sufficient to sustain the use of technology in teaching. Instructors must receive technical support in servicing equipment and software, media production, and instructional design. This needs to be done through the provision of technical and educational support close to departments, through the establishment of specialized central units, and through project management.

Copyright and ownership of materials needs to be understood and procedures put in place to ensure compliance with the law, without being so restrictive that it stifles all attempts to use technology for teaching. Institutions need to be careful to protect their rights and ensure that both the institution and the individuals involved in creating and delivering technology-based teaching and learning are properly rewarded for their efforts.

Finally, there is no point in pouring millions of dollars into infrastructure and computers and multimedia unless the faculty reward system is changed. The cultural change process must be recognized. The support of faculty members is critical for the adoption of new practices; hence, the cultural environment in which they work must be understood and sufficient support found to make teaching with technology both rewarding and interesting to them.

Chapter Six

Calculating the Costs of Teaching with Technology

There are fundamental differences between the cost structures of face-to-face and technology-based teaching. Indeed, cost structures of different technologies, such as videoconferencing, the Web, and CD-ROMs, vary considerably. This means that what may be cost-effective in one context—for example, a course with small annual enrollments—may be very different in another—for example, a course with large annual course enrollments. A basic understanding of the cost structures of technology-based teaching is essential to decision making.

Technology Costs

The heading has two meanings and both are relevant: first, technology costs lots of money, and second, a variety of costs are associated with the use of information technology at a university or college, some of which tend to be ignored, underestimated, or underbudgeted.

Analyzing Technology Costs

Technology costs can be broken down into a number of categories, including technology infrastructure, administrative applications, and academic applications.

I am primarily concerned in this book with the third area, the costs of academic applications. However, until quite recently technology investment has been driven primarily by administrative rather than academic requirements. Information systems were originally developed for student registration and records, financial tracking and management, and human resources management. Communications systems such as telephone and e-mail were also developed primarily for management and administrative purposes.

Although there has always been educational technology investment, some of a substantial nature—such as television studios—this has tended to be relatively independent of the main administrative systems. In the last few years, though, the development of the Internet and especially the World Wide Web has led to a considerable increase in the use of computers and networks for academic as well as administrative purposes. These academic applications tend to use the same or similar networks and systems as administrative applications.

This use of existing networks for academic applications has some advantages and some disadvantages. Infrastructure costs can be shared across a wider range of applications. However, as more and more use is made of information systems for educational purposes, capacity issues and conflict over priorities can arise. Administrative systems are primarily concerned with text and number crunching, and are not usually real-time related; in other words, data can be stored and forwarded to even out the traffic. Such systems may not be the best for educational purposes (which tend to be increasingly multimedia and hence real-time dependent).

Also, the true cost of educational applications may be hidden because the time instructors spend developing technology-based educational materials is not tracked or budgeted. Educational technology support costs may be underbudgeted because their importance is not understood or because such costs conflict with other funding priorities, such as research.

Thus, before looking at funding strategies it is important to get a general understanding of the nature of the costs of educational technologies and their relation to benefits.

Understanding the Human Nature of Cost Analysis

It may not come as a surprise to know that governments, educational institutions, and even the private sector are often prepared to invest many millions of dollars in information and communication technologies without any understanding or appreciation of the relationship between costs and performance. As Holt and Thompson (1998) point out: "It appears that investment in IT in universities is a highly politicized process often based at least partly on an act of faith that IT will help to deliver on the quality and productivity agenda. . . . Such investment processes and imperatives are not necessarily amenable to rationalistic cost-benefit investment models and techniques."

The lack of willingness of managers, researchers, and governments to develop and apply cost-benefit analysis to technology investment in education is a clear indicator that education is not a technical-rational activity but one in which mystique, prejudice, and ignorance sometimes rule—which is probably why we love it so much.

Yet cost analysis in this field is not rocket science. Compared with understanding human behavior or predicting the weather, cost analysis is relatively simple. Although costs vary from context to context, there is a well-defined underlying structure to technology costs, which enables reasonably accurate cost analyses to be made. Nevertheless, although costing exercises usually apply quantitative techniques, one should not be fooled by the apparent "scientific" nature of this process. All costing exercises depend on making certain assumptions. These assumptions are open to challenge.

Furthermore, costing activities are context-driven. What is treated as a cost in one organization may not be treated as a cost in another. Management can quite arbitrarily decide what constitutes a cost. For instance, in my university, videoconferencing facilities are not charged directly to departments wishing to use these services for teaching, whereas printing costs are.

There are always reasons why things are costed the way they are. The issue is whether they are good reasons. Furthermore, whether they are good reasons will depend on who you are and what decisions you have to make. The manager of a videoconferencing unit trying to keep staff fully employed and the facilities heavily used would not want to load all costs on to users, especially those costs (for example, salaries of regular staff) that have to be met whether or not the facility is used. In contrast, the vice president of information systems, who as a result of a university policy decision has to pay for all services from fees charged to users, may have a difference of opinion with the videoconferencing manager over his charging policy.

Note also in this case that the vice president of information systems may be enforcing a policy she does not agree with but which has been made at an even more senior management level. You are then right into the politics of an organization and the consistency or logic (or lack of it) in setting budgets and allocating costs. For instance, why in some institutions are information technology costs recharged to academic departments when library costs are not? One answer may be that library costs are considered a core academic function, while the institution has not yet in practice accepted information technology as having the same status.

All this is just another way of saying that it is important to think critically and analytically about the following costing methods and their application, because you may quite legitimately want to analyze costs using completely different assumptions.

Calculating the Costs of Teaching with Technology

This is a very brief introduction to a quite complex area (see Bates, 1995, and Rumble, 1997, for more information on costing methods). However, an understanding of key principles of costing new technologies for teaching is essential for decision making.

The most important distinction is between *fixed* and *variable* costs. Fixed costs do not change with student numbers, while variable costs do. One element of fixed costs is the cost of developing materials. Once a CD-ROM is designed and finished, that *development* cost is fixed, no matter how many students subsequently use it. However, the cost of *distributing* a CD-ROM is variable, because the more students, the more copies need to be made, and hence the higher the cost of duplication and distribution.

The costs of technology-based teaching differ fundamentally from the costs of face-to-face teaching in terms of the ratio of fixed to variable costs. In the conventional higher education model, costs have tended to increase with student numbers, or quality drops. In other words, if the student-teacher ratio is kept constant, more teachers are needed. If more teachers are not recruited, class size increases, interaction with the teacher drops, and quality declines.

Figure 6.1 shows the relationship between costs and student numbers for conventional classroom teaching with levels of teacher-student interaction kept constant. Costs increase as a step function. If the "target" teacher-student ratio is 1:20, then costs increase with each twenty students as an extra teacher is hired.

However, the cost structures for technology-based teaching are quite different. Technology-based courses cost a good deal of money up front to create, but once created many students can use them with relatively small increases in costs. Thus their fixed costs are high but their variable costs are low, in comparison with face-to-face teaching.

Figure 6.2 shows the relationship between the costs of classroom teaching and the costs of preprepared multimedia materials, such as a CD-ROM or a Web site.

Figure 6.1. Costs of Classroom Teaching.

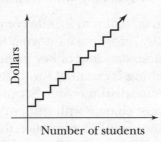

**Figure 6.2. Costs of Classroom Teaching
Versus Multimedia Materials.**

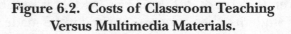
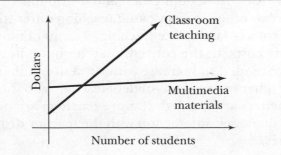

Original multimedia materials such as a CD-ROM created from scratch have a higher "starting" or fixed cost than classroom teaching, but after production the only additional costs are those of making and distributing compact discs (assuming that students already have their own computers and CD-ROM players).

Still, Figure 6.2 does not cover all the costs of technology-based teaching. Well-designed multimedia materials can both present information and provide a large amount of the interaction and feedback that would otherwise be provided by teachers. This frees up time for the teacher to concentrate just on those areas where person-to-person interaction is critical.

Computers are not smart enough, however, to anticipate all the questions, misunderstandings, and more important, original and creative outputs that students can generate. Thus, there is still the need for some provision not only for student-teacher interaction but also even more important for interaction between students. In the traditional face-to-face context this interaction is provided through small-group seminars. The equivalent in technology-based teaching is on-line discussion forums, such as computer conferencing. Thus, we have to consider not only the cost of preprepared multimedia materials but also the cost of on-line discussion and tutoring, as shown in Figure 6.3.

This figure indicates the cost of providing on-line student-teacher and student-student interaction (via computer conferencing, Arrow C). The costs of on-line interaction tend to be lower than those of conventional teaching as student numbers increase. This

Figure 6.3. Costs of Computer Conferencing.

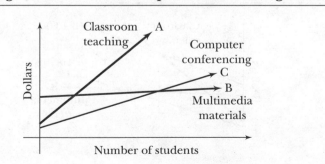

is because a good deal of the students' study time with technology-based learning is spent interacting with the preprepared multimedia material, so the teacher needs to spend less time per student overall moderating discussion forums compared with the total time spent in classroom teaching. However, the on-line costs still have to be added to the costs of preprepared multimedia materials, as shown in Figure 6.4 (Arrow D).

It can be seen in this model that for smaller numbers of students, conventional classroom teaching is likely to be less costly than preprepared multimedia and computer conferencing combined. However, as numbers increase the new media become increasingly more cost-effective.

The question on everyone's lips is: "What is the number of students at which technology-based teaching becomes more cost-effective than face-to-face teaching (point *y* in Figure 6.4)?" The unsatisfactory answer is: "Nobody knows for sure!"

At UBC we now have substantial cost and benefit data on the costs of developing and delivering face-to-face, print-based, video-conferencing, Web-based, and CD-ROM–based courses. We are fairly confident that a standard Web-based course, with a mix of preprepared Web materials, on-line discussion forums, and print in the form of required texts, becomes increasingly more cost-effective than face-to-face teaching as numbers per class increase beyond forty per year over a four-year period. This assumes that interaction between students and teachers remains high. Conversely, we tend to avoid developing distributed learning courses for fewer

**Figure 6.4. Costs of Classroom Teaching Versus
Multimedia and Computer Conferencing.**

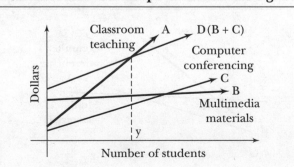

than twenty students per year. Between twenty and forty students per year per course, any cost differences are likely to be less significant than differences in benefits. For a CD-ROM–based course using lots of multimedia or expert systems, student numbers would need to be in the hundreds annually to become more cost-effective than classroom teaching.

Nevertheless, there is a great lack of hard data on actual costs, not only of the new media but even of conventional teaching in higher education. Much also depends on the design of technology-based teaching, the balance between preprepared material and on-line discussion forums, and the nature of the face-to-face teaching, such as the balance between large lecture classes and small seminar groups.

One commonly asked question is the ideal ratio of students to a tutor on an on-line course. The answer, of course, is that it all depends! The driving factor is the amount and nature of the interaction between the tutor and students. A course requiring didactic information transmission will have little need for teacher-student interaction, especially if the predesigned learning materials provide feedback, self-assessment tests, and so forth. We have one or two on-line courses of such a nature with one tutor to over a hundred students. Such a course will have high development or fixed costs and low marginal or variable costs, since the tutoring load is minimal.

Another course may require a high degree of student-student and student-teacher interaction because course content is open to different interpretations or needs to be related to highly variable individual student needs. Such a course might be based on readings and discussions. We have several graduate and professional courses of this kind, with fewer than ten students to a tutor. Such a course would have low development or fixed costs and high marginal or variable costs. For a course with a balanced mix of didactic teaching and on-line course discussion, we aim for a ratio of one on-line tutor to roughly twenty students.

It can be seen that the student-teacher ratio is as much determined by educational philosophy, course design, and student numbers as by technology. The point of this discussion is not so much to compare the costs of face-to-face and technology-based teaching as to show why an understanding of fixed and variable costs, and the differences in cost structure between face-to-face and technology-based teaching, is so important.

Allocating Costs

To emphasize this point, I will show how we calculate the costs of our Web-based courses and how we use this calculation to decide on appropriate student numbers, and for full cost-recovery courses, the appropriate fee to charge.

Overheads

A great difficulty in costing technologies is how to assign indirect costs or *overheads*. Overheads are various kinds of costs carried by an organization that are general and difficult to assign to a particular activity.

Buildings are one example of overheads for face-to-face teaching. There are two types of costs associated with buildings: *capital* and *operating*. Capital costs tend to be larger, once-only investments in equipment or facilities. The construction and fitting of a building is the obvious example of a fixed capital cost. *Operating* costs— the annual cost, for instance, of heating, cleaning, and maintaining a building—are recurrent costs, that is, they occur every year.

The standard way to handle capital costs for a building (or major equipment purchases) is to average or *amortize* the costs over the life of the investment by dividing the cost of the building by the number of years it will be used. This will give an annual amortized capital cost. If a building costs $1 million and is expected to last fifty years before being replaced, then the annual amortized cost would be $20,000 per annum. For a classroom building, given the number of students likely to use it over fifty years, the annual amortized capital cost per student is likely to be very small.

If the annual operating cost is added to the annual amortized capital cost, and the sum is divided by the number of users, an overhead cost per user per year can be calculated. This would enable an annual cost per student for use of a classroom building to be calculated. This overhead cost needs to be added to the direct costs of face-to-face teaching because classrooms are an essential requirement. Similarly, for the purpose of calculating capital costs for teaching with technology, the cost of the technology infrastructure would be considered an overhead because it is essential for the production and delivery of this type of teaching.

In addition to the costs of physical plant and infrastructure, there are staffing costs that can be considered as overheads. For instance, in my unit, as director, I am not usually directly involved in the production and delivery of courses. I am a general manager. In other words, I am an overhead cost to a particular course. The usual way of dealing with such overhead costs as my salary, benefits, travel, and so forth, is to average them out over each course, that is, to divide the costs by the number of courses generated. This seems reasonable for although I am not a direct cost for a course, my work is (I like to believe) essential for the development and delivery of distance education courses.

Furthermore, my unit is located in the Division of Continuing Studies, which has an associate vice president, a director of administration, and a number of central services such as marketing, accounts, and so on. The whole division is meant to balance its books. These overhead costs too are averaged out over the different units, including the Distance Education and Technology unit, roughly on a usage basis. For example, the accounts section of Continuing Studies estimates that our unit constitutes about 5 percent of their work, so we get "allocated" 5 percent of their costs, which we have to find from our budget.

In addition, there are a number of other overhead costs, such as computer provision and technical support (we pay about $40,000 per year, or $2,000 per staff member), telephone services, heating and lighting, and so on. Beyond that, there are a number of university central services that we have to cover, such as the central finance office, the president's office, and a whole host of other services, such as registration, human resources, and so on. Our total overheads this year paid from our budget to the university as a whole was $450,000 out of a total budget of $2.4 million—that is, almost 20 percent of our budget. However, without those central services it would be difficult for us to operate. If capital depreciation for buildings, the opportunity value of the land for other developments, and so on, were also included, our overheads would be even higher.

Three main options for handling overhead costs are:

- Not to charge users of the service for overheads (that is, ignore it for costing purposes)
- To average the overhead costs out over each operational function using the service (a cost per program or course using that service)
- To spread the costs over all operational units, whether they use the service or not

Which strategy to use in allowing for overhead costs depends on the type of decision to be made. For a university or college wanting to know whether to invest in a technology, it needs to include all overhead costs, probably adjusted to different bands of activity. It would be reasonable then to allocate these costs to all operational units that might use the technology for teaching purposes, whether they use it or not. When an institution invests in a technology, it should make an estimate of reasonable use, and charge an average cost to reflect that.

To compare the costs of classroom teaching with teaching with technology, it is important to include overhead costs. Overhead costs will differ between the two, and overhead or indirect costs may be more important than direct costs for assessing the costs and benefits of using information technology for teaching. Thus it is strongly recommended that overhead costs be assigned to courses or programs when doing cost analyses, and that these be averaged out over the potential users of the activity. If the overheads associated with the technology are high and the number of users low, this is an expensive technology, whether or not users are charged for the service.

Given the complexity of estimating and assigning overheads to teaching activities, it is not surprising that many institutions do not bother to assign overheads when costing courses. The overhead costs have to be paid and are often taken off the top. However, one advantage of allocating overheads to direct teaching activities is that it puts pressure on central units to keep down their costs. Once the operating units or faculties see what they must pay for central services such as accounting or technology networks, they often question the level of service being provided by central units. (This is called "whining" by central units, "gouging" by operating units, and "creative tension" by senior management.)

There is growing evidence from our cost studies that over-heads and central costs are a large proportion of the total teaching costs (over 50 percent for face-to-face teaching at UBC) and that there are differences in central services needed for face-to-face and technology-based teaching. Therefore, overheads should be calculated and assigned appropriately to courses when making comparisons.

Shared Costs

One difficulty in costing technologies for teaching is that the same service is often shared between quite different functional units. For instance, as already mentioned, computer services and networks are often shared between administrative and teaching units. If a network is already in place for administrative purposes, should not the initial investment and operational costs of the network be excluded from the teaching costs?

One way of handling this is to look at the marginal or additional costs of extending the network to teaching. However, technology investment is difficult to unbundle, in terms of function. For instance, at UBC students can register and pay their fees online as well as access their teaching over exactly the same network. It is extremely difficult to separate out the marginal costs of increasing campus network capacity by function and probably not worth the effort, unless one is interested in decisions such as whether to build more classrooms or handle expansion by more off-campus teaching. At that point, some kind of functional analysis of network costs does become worthwhile.

Identifying Basic Assumptions in Costing Exercises

I have gone through this somewhat complex analysis to indicate how important—and questionable—are the assumptions being made when costing teaching activities. It can be seen why different costing studies can come to completely different conclusions if the assumptions are different between the studies. However, this does not mean that the exercise is meaningless. What matters is that the assumptions be made clear so that alternative analyses can be made on different assumptions.

So, in summary:

- How fixed, capital, overheads, and shared costs are treated should depend on the decisions to be made and who is making the decisions.
- It is recommended that fixed capital technology costs for teaching services be calculated and assigned to all programs or courses that might be expected to use them, and that other overhead costs, as far as possible, also be calculated and assigned to courses and programs on the basis of whether the service is relevant to the needs of students and teachers using that technology.
- Where teaching shares networks and equipment installed for other purposes, shared costs should be treated as zero unless the marginal costs of using shared facilities for teaching are significant.

Costing a World Wide Web Program

As part of a national cost-benefit study of telelearning (NCE-Tele-learning), we have tracked the costs of developing a number of our Web-based courses. We were able to do this cost analysis partly because these courses had to recover fully their costs and partly because we had a researcher, Silvia Bartolic, who was able to collect data about the time spent by each of the people involved in developing and administering these courses.

The following example is from a postgraduate, one semester, thirteen-week distributed learning course offered over the Internet, requiring an estimated 130 to 150 hours of study. A Web site, which contained a range of resources including on-line discussion forums, formed the core of the course. Students, however, also required two textbooks and a set of selected readings collected together in the form of a print package, which were mailed to students, who purchased the print materials.

The course in this example is one of five offered internationally as part of a postgraduate certificate program aimed at working professionals. On-campus students at UBC could also take the courses, in distributed learning mode, as an elective within UBC's Master's of Education. The course was also "franchised" to Monterrey Institute of Technology (Monterrey Tech) in Mexico. Monterrey Tech enrolled its own students and provided tutoring and assessment of students, who took these courses as part of its Master's in Educational Technology. Although students enrolled through Monterrey Tech had their own discussion forums moderated by Monterrey Tech's own tutors, the content was the same as for the UBC registered students.

Hardware, Software, and Operational Costs

Web sites are created using special server software that employs the Hyper Text Transfer Protocol (HTTP). The most popular server software runs on UNIX or Windows NT computers.

Operation and maintenance of Web servers requires someone skilled in computer programming. Furthermore, anyone running a number of courses on a regular basis will need a reliable backup system, so that if a machine fails or requires servicing, there is a parallel service that can take over, enabling twenty-four-hour student access to be maintained.

There are several general approaches to developing Web courses. One common approach is to use HTML to construct Web pages "by hand." Another is to use an integrated Web application (such as WebCT), which can assist the author in all levels of a site's content management and creation.

An organization offering on-line courses will want a system that is as simple and as reliable as possible for those using it in order to avoid high student technical training and support costs.

Student technical support costs can be reduced if students themselves are responsible for obtaining access to the Internet, either through a university's own service or through a local Internet service provider. For the professional courses we are costing, we assumed that students already had a computer and Internet access. We do not teach students how to use the computer, either.

This approach may not be suitable for other contexts, such as schools, courses aiming to teach students how to use a computer, or inexperienced computer users. In such cases, student technical support costs are likely to be much higher. We also benefitted from the technical support services provided by UBC's campus computer and communications division, as well as from services provided by the library at UBC, which runs courses for students on how to use the Internet for study purposes. These costs are not included.

We have chosen in our Distance Education and Technology unit (DET) to install and run our own suite of servers, and that has required employing highly skilled Internet specialists who are much more expensive than a graduate student helper. On the other hand, our student technical support costs are low (we get very few technical problems with our courses in terms of system operation). Also, the initial high cost of servers and the Internet specialists can be averaged across the growing number of on-line courses we are offering, and even more important, can be set off against the very large savings from not having to provide extensive student technical help services.

Student Costs

Probably the most important feature of the Web is that it provides "standard" software for end users. In other words, if students have Netscape or Explorer browsers, they have the potential to access anything on the Web. Furthermore, for educational use these browsers are free. For these courses, we originally used off-the-shelf software called HyperNews for our discussion groups. This is free for educational users, although it requires skill in UNIX programming. Provided we design our own Web sites and use free software available over the Web, we have no site license or software costs to carry and neither do our students. We have since switched to using WebCT for these courses, but the costing for this example has been done on the original system.

Systems such as WebCT that do require a site license are also relatively cheap for educational institutions (go to http://home-brew.cs.ubc.ca/webct/get/pricing.html to see the pricing structure). In contrast, the Lotus Notes educational software for developing courses, Learning Space, is much more expensive for end users and more complex to learn. This is one reason we do not use it, although in contexts such as business networks or business courses where users already have Lotus Notes installed for other purposes, it may be a viable option.

For these five postgraduate courses we expected students already to have their own computers. Students accessed the courses from home or work through the Internet. Many of the students in these courses were working or studying at other universities and thus had no difficulty in using their office computer or using computers in local computer labs.

Costs Over the First Year of a Course

There are several ways to calculate costs:

- Wild guesses ("It costs about the same/more/less for a distance course as a face-to-face course"; "Web courses are about two-thirds the cost of a print-based course"; "Oh, I guess we spend about $10,000 a course")
- Marginal costs, which may reflect just the cash or extra costs needed to put on a course but exclude fixed costs and staff salaries
- Careful estimates of full cost based on experience, including overheads
- Actual costs, as measured by the actual time and money spent on the course, and including overheads

The numbers shown in Table 6.1 are careful full-cost estimates.

Let us look at these costs line by line. It should be noted that all dollars shown are Canadian unless otherwise stated.

Subject Experts

Subject experts at $400 a day ($280 in U.S. dollars) is based on two hundred working days a year (removing weekends, holidays, and so on) and including all benefits for an average salary of $80,000 ($56,000 U.S.). This is a graduate course taught by staff in the higher range of academic salaries.

Some would argue that this cost should be excluded because salaries are a fixed cost. However, these courses were new and did not replace an existing program, and because different technologies demand different amounts of time from subject experts it is important to include this cost.

The academic time is also a little high because the estimate included new curriculum development; adapting an existing

Table 6.1. Costs of EDST 565f in the First Year.

Fixed Costs	Dollars
Subject experts (30 days @ C$400 per day)	12,000
Internet specialist (7 days @ C$300 per day)	2,100
Graphics and interface design (4 days @ C$300 per day)	1,200
Copyright clearance	700
Direct DET costs	16,000
DET overheads @ 25% of $16,000	4,000
Library	1,000
Server costs	300
International tutors (3 @ C$1,000)	3,000
Faculty of education academic approval	4,000
Total fixed costs	28,300

Variable Costs	
Tutoring (40 students @ $220 per student)	8,800
Delivery costs	
Noncredit registration ($14.00 × 29)	406
Student administration ($28.86 × 40)	1,155
Printed materials including postage ($37.50 × 40)	1,500
Total variable costs	11,861
Total costs to UBC (fixed and variable)	40,161

Costs to Students	UBC Graduate Students	Certificate/ Noncredit
Fees	463	695
Required readings	177	177
Postage	0	15–100
Internet access	15	21–50
Computer	0	0

Note: Table shows UBC costs only. Dollars shown are Canadian; C$1.00 = U.S. $0.67.

curriculum would have been less costly in academic time. However, the subject experts in this case were experienced in using the technology; new users will take much longer to develop their first course using a new technology.

Internet Specialist, Graphics and Interface Design

In order to ensure easy navigation of the course, a "clean" look, and minimum download speeds, input from an Internet specialist and a graphics and interface design specialist is strongly recommended for all on-line courses, whether using off-the-shelf software such as WebCT or not. This course was what we call a "roll-your-own" HTML course. In other words, we designed the interface because with different groups of students registered with ITESM in Mexico and with UBC, we could not at the time use a standard interface. Also, when the first course was designed, most off-the-shelf packages were still in a developmental stage. Designing our own interface also had the advantage of not having to pay software license fees.

On this course, three *international guest tutors* (including the authors of the required textbooks) were invited to moderate a discussion for a week each. However, this did not replace regular tutoring activity and so was an additional cost.

Normally for courses developed by our unit, there would be an additional line item for *project management–instructional design*. However, unusually, the subject experts also happened to be project managers–instructional designers by background, so this is rolled into subject expert costs. Normally, this would be a separate line item (we would allow a maximum of ten days or $4,000 for a one-semester course for this function).

Copyright Clearance

Copyright clearance was required for the collection of printed custom course materials (selected journal articles or chapters from books) that accompanied the course.

DET Costs

DET overheads covered the overheads referred to earlier, including a charge from UBC's central computers and communications division for network access, and for the costs of staff workstations.

Library

The UBC library provided two services to the course. A librarian was a member of the course team and helped identify relevant readings (both printed and on-line) for the course, and UBC students could go on-line to the library catalogues and order any journal articles or books, which, for a small fee, were faxed or mailed to students.

Server

Server costs are amortized over three years, the average life of a computer these days. We have two servers—one a backup—at a total cost of $9,000. We are developing approximately ten new Web courses a year, or thirty over three years, so the average cost per course is $9,000 ÷ 30 = $300. Even this cost is probably too high, because the servers are used for other purposes besides course development and delivery.

Academic Approval

There was for this course a charge of $4,000 from the Faculty of Education for their costs in giving academic approval to this course. This is an unusual cost (some would say cruel and unusual), because if the course had been developed in the Faculty of Education (or any other faculty), this cost would have been zero. However, it does compensate for the time spent by academics in the faculty on reviewing and approving the educational quality of the courses.

Tutoring

Tutor costs are based on an estimate of actual time spent tutoring this course, including moderating on-line discussions, dealing with e-mail from students and the course team, and marking assignments, averaged across each student. On this particular course, there were three tutors team-tutoring (the instructors who designed and developed the course) with a tutor-student ratio of 1:13. This may seem high for a graduate course, but ten of the forty students were auditing, taking the course but not submitting assignments or being graded.

Delivery

Delivery costs are based on the average costs, developed over a large number of courses, for registering and administering distance education students. Note that registration costs exclude the UBC graduate students, who were already registered before this course began. Their registration costs are covered in the overheads charged by the university to our unit on credit student tuition fees.

The *variable* cost to UBC for each student is $300 ($220 for tutoring plus $80 for materials and administration). This is also the marginal cost to UBC of adding another student to the course. If we added in the $177 that the student pays for printed materials, the total variable cost per student would be $477, plus any computer and communications costs that the student bears.

Revenues

We should also look at *revenues*. For every graduate student on a three-credit master's course, our unit receives $463 from UBC graduate tuition revenues. For the certificate and noncredit students, these courses have to be self-financing, because the provincial government does not subsidize noncredit programming. We therefore set a charge of $695 for the certificate and noncredit students (see the next section on pricing policies). We also received payment from Monterrey Tech for half the cost of development, but this has not been included in these calculations.

Students' Costs

In addition to the fees, students pay the full cost of printed materials. For EDST 565f, there were two set books, costing a total of $120, plus the custom course materials at $56.65 a set, plus postage (an average of $15 for Canadian students and $30 for international students, although the costs varied a great deal, as some students paid courier fees).

Finally, students have to find the cost of a computer and Internet access. These are very difficult to allocate, particularly if a student has a computer for other purposes, where the marginal cost for this course might be considered zero. The cost of Internet access varies also, from as low as $15 a month to over $50 a month, depending on location.

I have gone through these costs in detail so that it can be seen how they were derived. This illustrates the point that costing is like playing golf. If you cheat, it is between you and God—no one else is likely to know! It does demand self-discipline and honesty to ensure that all costs are included.

However, we are not ready yet to calculate average costs, because we have to look at the costs over the life of the course, and not just in the first year in which it is offered.

Costs Over the Life of a Course

We do not know yet what the life of EDST 565f will be, but I expect it will have four presentations (one a year over four years). I have also assumed that the course will continue to enroll forty students per year.

With print-based courses, we spend about 10 percent of the original development cost per year in maintaining and updating courses. However, with Web-based courses this maintenance cost is usually higher because the subject experts are continually adding and replacing Web sites, references, readings, and so forth. I have assumed then a maintenance cost of 33 percent, or ten days per year of subject expert time.

The Internet specialist spent two days setting up the site and the equivalent of five days maintaining it in the first year. He is also likely to have to spend the equivalent of five days per year maintenance on this course during each presentation. The graphics and interface designer will need to spend one day making minor corrections or changes to the course in the second year, taking into account student and tutor feedback, but it should remain stable after that. Copyright, though, will have to be paid each year for reproducing the readings.

There was a one-off cost for the services of the librarian in the first year for helping to locate appropriate readings. Similarly, the fixed costs of the server were written off in the first year. In contrast, the international tutors need to be paid each year. Faculty approval is also a one-time cost per course. Tutoring and delivery costs will be constant over the four years, provided student enrollments stay the same each year.

Using these assumptions, I have broken down the likely costs as follows (see Table 6.2):

The total cost then of this course over four years is $108,209 ($75,746 U.S.) for a total of 160 students (4 × 40).

Once we have the full costs of a course at this level of detail, we can start doing some useful calculations, depending on our purpose. Indeed, we can now start changing some assumptions, thus "modeling" costs.

Table 6.2. Costs of EDST 565f Over Four Years.

	Year 1	Year 2	Year 3	Year 4	Total Dollars
Fixed Costs					
Subject experts	12,000	4,000	4,000	4,000	24,000
Internet specialist	2,100	1,500	1,500	1,500	6,600
Design	1,200	300	0	0	1,500
Copyright	700	700	700	700	2,800
Subtotal	16,000	6,500	6,200	6,200	34,900
DET overheads	4,000	1,625	1,550	1,550	8,725
Library	1,000	0	0	0	1,000
Server	300	0	0	0	300
International tutors	3,000	3,000	3,000	3,000	12,000
Faculty approval	4,000	0	0	0	4,000
Total fixed	28,300	11,125	10,750	10,750	60,925
Variable Costs					
Tutoring	8,800	8,800	8,800	8,800	35,200
Delivery	3,021	3,021	3,021	3,021	12,084
Total variable	11,821	11,821	11,821	11,821	47,284
Total all costs	40,121	22,946	22,571	22,571	108,209

Note: Table shows UBC costs only. Dollars shown are Canadian;
C$1.00 = U.S. $0.67.

Calculating Total Costs

I will continue to use EDST 565f as an example.

Average Cost per Student

The easiest cost to calculate is the average cost per student. The average cost per UBC student in the first year appeared to be $1,003 ($40,121 ÷ 40). However, the true average cost over four years is $676 ($108,209 ÷ 160), or $473 U.S. (If you were wondering how we set the student fee for certificate students at $695, now you know!) These are the costs, of course, to UBC. If one added in the printed materials that the student pays for, the total average cost is approximately $850, plus any computer and communications costs.

Each time the course is offered, the average cost per student comes down, so the life of the course, or the number of times it is offered, is significant. This is one indication of how the costs of technology-based teaching differ from face-to-face teaching.

Total Costs

The total costs over the four years at forty students a year was $108,209.

Pricing and Paying for Courses

Perhaps the most important decision that needs to be made when choosing technologies is how to calculate the price of a course so that costs are covered (or exceeded) by revenues or income.

In education and training there are several potential sources of funding: grants or subsidies from government or an employer, student fees, secondary sales of materials, franchising or copyright (fees paid by another organization in order to use the materials or offer the course), and advertising or sponsorship. For this exercise, I will assume that a course must at least cover all its costs from student fees. Three variables will affect whether this can be achieved: the cost of the course, the number of (paying) students, and the level (or price) of the fee.

We can vary each of these three variables and still achieve full cost recovery. For instance, if we know the likely number of students and the maximum they are likely to pay, we can calculate how much (or little) the production and delivery of the course must cost, as follows:

$$\text{COST OF COURSE} = \text{STUDENT NUMBERS} \times \text{COST OF FEES}$$

If we know how much the course will cost, and the maximum fee we can charge, we can work out how many students will be needed to break even, as follows:

$$\text{NUMBERS OF STUDENTS} = \text{COST OF COURSE} \div \text{COST OF FEE}$$

And if we know the cost of the course and the likely number of students, we can work out the optimum student fee to cover costs, as follows:

$$\text{STUDENT FEE} = \text{TOTAL COSTS} \div \text{NUMBER OF STUDENTS}$$

Last, we can vary all three, or model different scenarios. Usually when designing a course, you have to play around with all three variables, which is where the cost of using particular technologies becomes critical.

By building a model of costs around these three variables, it is possible to develop the financial elements of a business plan that can help decide whether to go ahead with the development of a particular course.

Taking EDST 565f as an example, we worked out how many full fee-paying students were needed to make this course viable, because access issues and teaching requirements largely determined the technologies. Also, our on-campus, face-to-face certificate programs were charging about $700 per course. This is how we did it:

$$\text{IF STUDENT NUMBERS} = \text{TOTAL COSTS} \div \text{COST OF FEE},$$
$$\text{THEN STUDENT NUMBERS} = \$108,209 \div 695.$$
$$\text{THIS COMES TO 156 STUDENTS OVER FOUR YEARS,}$$
$$\text{OR 39 STUDENTS PER YEAR.}$$

We did in fact get forty fee-paying students in the first year (although not all were full fee paying, as eleven were master's students, but they are also subsidized through government grant).

This is a very useful technique when assessing what technologies to use, or even more important, whether to go ahead with course production or not.

Developing In-House On-Line Courses Versus Outsourcing

A good arrangement for an individual or an organization wanting to run only one or two courses is to contract out the work as long as the external contractor can provide a high-quality and completely reliable service. Indeed, it is possible to hire commercial organizations such as e-College.com to develop and host a whole course.

Outsourcing is not such a good arrangement for an organization that is developing a large number of its own courses. Different courses require different designs, and one single authoring system may not be able to cope with this variety. Furthermore, an organization running a large number of on-line courses will want to ensure that the service is completely reliable, and will want easy access to the host server so that changes can be made and the priority of the organization in getting those changes made is met.

For small or medium-size universities, the decision about whether to outsource can be difficult. A number of factors have to be taken into account besides costs. If technology-based teaching is seen as core and central to the activities of the institution, it is probably advisable for it to develop its own in-house capacity. An organization with an already existing and competent in-house capacity and a large number of courses to develop would be better to support the internal unit than to contract in from outside. In contrast, an institution may have in-house capacity but it may not be cost-efficient, or it may be unresponsive to internal clients, or it may not be able or willing to adapt to changes in new technologies. These may all be reasons for bypassing the internal unit and outsourcing. However, if an agency external to the institution is to be contracted, then costs need to be examined carefully. What may look like a good deal may on closer examination prove to be an expensive option.

First, there is the issue of quality. What is included in the contract? For instance, will the external contractor provide instructional design, and a range of options and advice on software, teaching methods, and delivery? Will the materials be tailored to the needs of off-campus or distance students? Will the contracted service include interface design, and navigation tools, so that students can easily find their way round the course?

Second, who is going to do the bulk of the work? Who has to pull together all the material to be put on the Web site, get it into a suitable format, and clear copyright? If this is not to be done by the service provider, then major costs will fall on the academic staff or teaching department.

Third, does the contract permit changes to be made at a reasonable cost? For instance, if alterations or additional materials are necessary during the first offering of the course, is there an extra charge for this? If so, what will it be? (Some contracts require the same fee for any alterations as for the original work.) Who is responsible for checking the accuracy and reliability of the work, and for making changes and course maintenance, and how quickly can changes be made?

Fourth, who is responsible for tutoring? How will this be paid for? For instance, some contractors charge a low initial cost to put information up on the Web but then charge $100 (U.S. dollars) for every student. The economic benefit of this to the outsourcing institution will depend to some extent on the level of tuition fees that can be charged, and how they can be used. For instance, government sets tuition fees for undergraduate courses in British Columbia at roughly $250 ($175 U.S.) per three-credit course. The Distance Education and Technology unit at UBC gets these fees and uses them to pay for the cost of reproducing and delivering materials to students (print, mailing). We also use funds from fees to pay tutors, who mark assignments and assess students. The fee more or less balances the direct marginal cost per student. A department using an outside contractor to develop a course would have a major problem, even if allowed to keep the $250 tuition fee. It would not be able to cover even the cost of tuition ($180 per student or $120

U.S.), after paying $150 per student ($100 U.S.) to the external contractor.

Finally, what counts as a direct cost for in-house production and where does it come from? Contracting out may save costs on internal course developers but is likely to increase the work for academics, depending on the external contract and the service provided. Furthermore, the university provides money off the top for distance education course development at UBC, which includes paying for the time of the academic to work on on-line courses. Why would a department pay out hard cash to an external contractor and still have to do a major part of the work when it can receive additional internal funds for developing the course in house? However, the provost may want to compare the costs of external contractors with in-house services. At that level, outsourcing may look to be a better deal, particularly if there is no in-house service or if the in-house service seems inefficient or expensive to run.

In the end, it is likely to come down to quality rather than cost. External contractors tend to "cream" the easy work. Putting materials already created for classrooms up on to the Web is the easy part. Adapting or creating original materials that exploit on-line use, developing an institutional look and feel, putting in and running effective discussion forums, and providing quality tutoring and assignment marking are all labor-intensive and expensive. If external contractors can do all these things more cheaply and better than an in-house team, then it would make sense to outsource. Whatever the circumstances, a careful cost-benefit analysis at an institutional and departmental level should be done before outsourcing.

Technology as Classroom Aid

It is much easier to identify the costs of delivering teaching entirely at a distance through new technologies because it can be isolated as a relatively separate activity. It is much more difficult to calculate the costs of using technology to support regular classroom teaching, because it becomes so integrated with other regular costs.

Traditional teaching in higher education comes with a very high proportion of indirect costs. The Budget and Planning Office at UBC has done a detailed breakdown of the direct and indirect costs of teaching there. Indirect costs (buildings, central services such as the registry, the president's office, sewage, taxes, the library, general administration, information technology services, and so forth) when loaded back on a per-student basis constitute 53 percent of general-purpose operating funds. Thus, after stripping out research costs (and allocating their share of indirect costs), salaries of faculties and faculty support staff constitute only 47 percent of the operating funds spent on teaching.

The costs of technology supporting classroom teaching, such as the development of Web sites, are buried within the salaries and time of instructors and research students, as well as clearly identified educational technology support staff (direct costs), and within the technology infrastructure costs (indirect costs). To assess the real cost of the use of technology for supporting classroom teaching, these costs need to be identified. However, few higher education institutions have financial systems in place that enable this analysis to be done easily.

Nevertheless, some conclusions can be drawn.

- If the use of technology to support classroom technology does not result in savings in other activities, then costs will inevitably increase.
- It has proved difficult to show a direct relationship between increased learning performance and increased use of technology to supplement classroom teaching (this issue will be discussed in more detail in Chapter Nine).
- By far the largest cost in using technology to supplement classroom teaching is the time spent by instructors and their research students in developing PowerPoint presentations, Web sites, CD-ROMs, and so on.
- We have seen in Chapter Five that to make better use of faculty members' time and skills, more technical support is required than has been provided in most institutions to date. This will lead to further increases in cost, although increased research output and greater learning gains may compensate for this. However, there is little research evidence to date to support (or refute) this assumption.

- Finally, the impact of using new technologies to support classroom teaching is an area where research is urgently needed, an issue that is also discussed in more detail in Chapter Nine.

Putting in Appropriate Financial Systems

Most university and college financial systems are what might be termed *expenditure-driven*. Allocations of resources (mainly teaching and support staff) are made to faculties, and hence to departments, and the financial system tracks whether expenditures are consistent with allocations for salaries, benefits, expenses, materials, and so on. These budget lines are not related to specific activities, such as the cost of teaching a particular course. It is thus impossible to use financial reports based on an expenditure-driven model to analyze the costs of different courses, or different delivery mechanisms.

In addition, most publicly funded institutions until recently have received their funds in the form of a block "general purpose operating grant" from government, which is then broken down into smaller blocks for each faculty and then for each department. In many institutions, student fees are collected centrally and then reallocated as part of the block grant, independently of the courses or departments that generated the revenues. Consequently, there is often a single "target" figure for expenditure, and university and college accounts are not physically structured to account for and track revenues from multiple sources.

Because at UBC we still have an expenditure-based financial system, I have to keep two separate but related sets of accounts. One is the "university-divisional" set, and the other is the set I use for tracking the expenditures and revenues for each of the over one hundred projects or courses we have at any one time. The data for our project-based accounts all have to be entered separately, by my staff, but at the end of the day the totals of expenditures and revenues across the projects have to balance with the figures in the university's expenditure-driven accounts. This is a hugely inefficient system.

This is not specifically a problem caused by technology-based teaching; it applies particularly to cost-recovery units such as continuing studies or extension divisions that depend on tracking revenues as well as expenditures and need to know which activities or projects are breaking even, losing money, or making a profit.

It is also a problem with a solution. There are now administrative software systems available based on relational databases that allow the same data to be entered and analyzed locally for both expenditure-driven and activity-based accounting. However, there is a very high initial cost in researching and installing such systems.

Nevertheless, such systems will become increasingly necessary if institutions are to understand and control the costs of technology-based teaching. Despite the hazards involved in costing technology-based teaching (or teaching of any kind, for that matter), it will become increasingly important to put in place financial systems that allow expenditures and revenues to be tracked and allocated accurately on an activity basis. Only in this way will managers be able to make accurate assessments of the costs of different kinds of teaching. Without such activity-based financial systems, for instance, the decision to outsource or not will be purely subjective.

Conclusions

It is worth remembering the story about the company that was appointing a new chief accountant. Each candidate was asked a set of questions by the interviewing committee. The owner of the company asked only one question of each candidate, right at the end of the interview: "What's two plus two?" Each of the candidates looked puzzled and answered, "Four." When the last candidate came in, the owner again waited until the end and asked his question: "What's two plus two?" "What would you like it to be?" replied the candidate. He got the job.

One would like to think that there are more ethics in education and training than in business accountancy. However, as with all jokes, there is a point to the story. How one costs teaching by technology will depend on the kind of decisions to be made and what your position is in the decision-making chain. What is important is that all costs be identified, that the assumptions underlying the costings be transparent and understood, and that reasons for including or excluding the various cost lines or headings be valid for the purpose of the exercise.

What cost data we have suggests that the direct costs of well-managed technology-based teaching compare increasingly favorably with the direct costs of well-managed face-to-face teaching, particularly as student numbers for a particular course or program increases.

What we do not yet know is the impact of technology-based teaching on indirect costs or indirect benefits. There is some evidence that technology-based teaching could have significant potential advantages over face-to-face teaching when it comes to indirect costs and benefits. For instance, distributed learning could lead to reduced demand for new buildings, reductions in traffic to and from campus, and widening access to new target groups of learners. What we need are better methodologies and better financial systems for tracking revenues and expenditures, and more studies on the costs and benefits of both face-to-face and technology-based teaching.

Chapter Seven

Funding Strategies, Collaboration, and Competition

How can universities and colleges find resources to fund technology for teaching at a time when they are under increasing pressure to reduce costs, and when government grants are being cut? This is perhaps the most difficult of all the issues surrounding the use of technology for teaching.

There are several funding strategies to be considered:

- Using external grants for specific technology projects
- Charging student technology fees
- Increasing general operating grants from government to support the use of technology for teaching
- Reallocating internal funds
- Centralizing or decentralizing funding
- Balancing funding between infrastructure, administrative applications, and educational applications

Building partnerships, strategic alliances, or consortia with and between other public sector or private sector organizations is another strategy that is being used increasingly to share or reduce costs and fight off perceived competition.

Funding Strategies

The acquisition and allocation of resources is probably the most fundamental driver of change available to management. There are several approaches to this issue.

Special External Funding for Technology-Based Teaching

Special government funding to encourage technological innovation for teaching has prompted many universities and colleges to move more vigorously into the use of technology for teaching. The government of Alberta in Canada for instance has an "envelope" of funding held back to encourage innovation, which is applied for on a grant basis by individual faculty and instructors. Preference is given to proposals that foster interinstitutional collaboration.

Earmarked government funding is a good strategy to get institutions to pay attention to using technology for teaching, particularly if the money is taken from what they would otherwise have been allocated. This was the main stimulus that prompted the University of British Columbia to move into technology-based teaching in a systematic way in 1994–95.

However, there are also disadvantages or limitations to such a strategy. The first, of course, is that this interferes with the autonomy of the institution to make the most appropriate strategic decisions about where to invest resources. Indeed, a strategy such as the government of Alberta's can actually undermine an institution's attempt to manage its technological resources cost-effectively. Giving grants on an individual faculty or project basis, by criteria determined by government, makes it more difficult for an institution to control or manage the direction of its use of technology for teaching toward wider strategic purposes.

Furthermore, if the argument is accepted that technology will be more effectively used if we follow the principles of successful, postindustrial, information-based organizations, then government management is a crude strategy, too far removed from the action. Government officials are unlikely to have the expertise to be able to make judgments about the quality and likely impact of the individual grant proposals received. Nor are they in a position to judge the appropriate amount of funding needed to bring about significant change in the system.

Therefore, a common solution is to establish an advisory committee, probably drawn from academics in the various institutions, to adjudicate on the bids. However, such committees will have just as much difficulty in identifying strategic uses for such funds at a system level, and they can easily degenerate into protecting narrow institutional interests or horse-trading.

Another strategy, particularly popular in institutions in the United States, is to rely on grants from external organizations, such as the Department of Education, research councils, state "special accounts," charities or private endowments, and increasingly, corporate sponsorship. Again, the value of this type of funding is a question of timing. It can be a very good stimulus for getting institutions started in using technologies, as they do not have to give up anything to do it. It can also be useful to supplement or enhance other activities already funded by the institution. There is less risk attached to this kind of funding. If the project does not produce the results hoped for, the institution is not committed to continuing the activity.

However, by its nature, such funding is limited in duration. It raises the question of sustainability. What happens when the funds run out? Successful projects then become a real problem. How does the institution continue or extend the project? Second, staff who work on such projects tend to be employed on a temporary basis. When the project ends, they leave, and thus the learning experience and wisdom gained from the project is lost to the institution. Because the new technologies for teaching present new challenges, there are proportionately few professionals with good experience and knowledge in this field. It is therefore all the more important that there is continuity and a chance to gain knowledge and experience and retain that in an organization committed to the use of technology for teaching. Short-term funding makes this difficult, if not impossible. Third, externally funded projects can float along on the sidelines, without affecting the core activities of the institution. They can be safely ignored, whether or not they are successful.

The biggest danger, though, of short-term external funding or corporate partnerships is that the institution has less control over its own fate. It becomes increasingly driven by short-term opportunities and other organizations' agendas. Government priorities change. The board or chief executive officer of a foundation may change, with different interests. Private sector partners need to see some return on their investment, and they will pull out if their objectives are not being met in the way anticipated.

Thus, although special external funding can be very useful, it should not be the only strategy for an institution, and an institution's management needs to ensure as far as it can that such grants integrate with the wider plans and directions for the institution.

Student Technology Fees

Many institutions are now passing some of the costs of technology investment directly on to the students by means of a student technology fee.

Sonoma State has introduced a student technology fee that applies to all students, as well as requiring students to provide their own computers. The fee is used to provide technical help and support for students, to improve the local area network, to provide docking ports for laptops, and to make available easy access to public computers in public places on campus. Students themselves play a large role in managing this fund and in approving the level of the fee. Collège Boréal levies a fee of $1,200 ($800 in U.S. dollars) per student per year. Each student gets a laptop computer on lease, with the option of buying it at a much reduced price after two years.

However, students will vote in favor of such a fee (as they did at both Sonoma State and Collège Boréal) only if the benefits to them are clear. In particular, the institution needs to make very clear the added value to students of using computers for learning. Furthermore, charging students an additional fee for technology access, even if it leads to more equitable access, seems questionable to me. Quite apart from the issues around escalating costs to students caused by creeping supplementary fees, there is a wider principle here. We do not charge students in most institutions for access to the library or for the use of lecture halls. What is the difference in principle that requires them to pay extra for technology access?

Nevertheless, there are several reasons why a growing number of institutions are imposing special student technology fees. The first is that the need for students to access computers for study purposes is "new." Because there is no existing budget for this, it is necessary to find a way to raise the money. Students are also likely to agree to this because they believe that the use of computers in their teaching is important. In other words, it is easier to sell an increase in fees for this specific purpose than a general fee increase. Another reason is that the institution has not accepted the use of technology for teaching as a core academic activity; it is supplementary and optional.

None of these explanations seems convincing to me. Students think it important enough to be willing to pay an additional fee that is often substantial, but the institution does not think it important enough to cover the costs fully from general purpose operating funds. It is understandable that at a time when state grants are declining, institutions look to tuition fee increases to pay for innovations. However, I see no reason why technology should be isolated as a special case for tuition increases.

Too often technology implementation is driven by temporary grant funding from foundations or corporate interests, or by special funding arrangements, such as student technology fees. If an institution sees the use of technology for teaching as critical for its development, then funds for implementing this should come from base operating funds.

Additional Government Funding for Technology

One could argue that the aim of using technology is to improve the quality of learning and to prepare students better for a knowledge-based society, rather than to save money. Governments then have a responsibility to face up to the additional costs that follow from committing to the use of technology for teaching.

However, the dominant political ideology in many jurisdictions in the United States, Canada, Australia, and Britain over the last decade has been to reduce rather than increase government funding on a per student basis. Institutions are often left with no alternative but to reallocate funds to provide the necessary support for teaching with technology.

Reallocating Funds

In the end, if teaching with technology is to be a key component of the institution, then the institution has to build it into its base operating budget.

Figure 7.1 depicts a theoretical or idealized strategy for funding reallocations at a universitywide level.

In year one, the institution is spending all its funds for teaching on classroom instruction. In year two, the government holds back 1 percent of the institution's grant for an innovation fund,

Figure 7.1. Reallocation Strategy for Academic Funding.

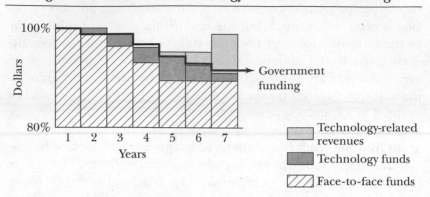

which the institution receives for identified specific technology applications for which the money will be used. In year three, the government withdraws the earmarked funds and in fact reduces the institution's operating grant by 1 percent. However, the institution was so impressed by the impact of the previous year's funding for technology-based teaching that it decides to find 2 percent from its own funds for such a purpose. Between years two and five, despite cuts in overall levels of funding, an increasing proportion of the base operating budget is allocated to the development of technology-based teaching despite steadily decreasing government funding.

However, also in year five we see a small increase in overall revenues due to a combination of increased enrollments and sales of learning materials flowing from earlier investments in technology-based teaching. This return on earlier investment continues and increases in years six and seven, until by year seven funds are almost back to year one levels, despite continued government funding cuts. Also, in year six the university decides to stabilize the level of funding for face-to-face teaching, assuming that any further decrease would be out of balance with its overall teaching goals.

Although a hypothetical example, at least the early years shown in the figure are not too far from fact. In 1994–95 the British Columbian government withheld 1 percent of all postsecondary institutions' operating budgets, and 0.5 percent in 1995–96, to be reclaimed by an institution if it came up with proposals for innovative teaching. In UBC's case, this came to approximately $4 million (Canadian) over the two years. UBC decided to use half this fund for campus technology infrastructure improvements, and the other half for technology-based teaching applications, with a small amount held back for establishing a small Center for Educational Technology. For 1996–97, when the government discontinued its innovation fund strategy (and did not restore the funding to the previous level), the university itself increased the level of funding for its own Teaching and Learning Enhancement Fund to $2.2 million (Canadian), to which individual faculty members could apply.

The willingness to reallocate funds is not only a necessary strategy if technology-based teaching is to become a core part of a university or college's operation but also a measure of the level of commitment to the concept by different organizational units. Eventually, funding reallocation will need to be pushed down to the faculty or even departmental level.

However, institutions that decide to do this will face some very difficult decisions in a "zero balance" or declining budget context. If increased investment in technology is necessary and budgets are constant, then something has to give. Some institutions have managed to make the technology investment through short-term funding from a variety of sources, but we have seen the dangers in relying on that kind of funding. Others have looked to increased revenues from increased enrollments, franchises, and sales of materials, as outlined in Figure 7.1. This is certainly possible, but there is a worrying lag between expenditure on technology-based teaching and revenue return.

Reorganization of existing resources may appear to be a better option than reallocation. Ancillary or support units such as the distance education department, the faculty development office, audiovisual services, some areas of computer services, and so on, may be reorganized to provide more support for teaching with technology throughout the university.

The danger in this approach is that although it may be necessary, it may not be sufficient. If these areas have been providing a good service before reorganization, they may not be able to cope, even after reorganization, with a major expansion in technology-based teaching without additional funding. This approach may have the appearance of bold action but may not make much difference in actual outcomes.

I am not arguing that one *should* close down teaching programs to support technology investment. However, an institution making a strategic commitment to the use of technology for teaching, with no external or additional resources to pay for such changes, must be prepared to consider closing programs and activities that are costly and relatively ineffective in order to pay for the new investment. This is the Faustian contract. Indeed, we may well see universities and colleges becoming less universal in their programming, concentrating their resources, including technology investment, on those areas giving the institution its greatest competitive advantage.

This may seem dire, but it is not an issue specific to technology. In a flat or declining funding context, *any* change that requires investment will have to be paid for by reallocations from some existing activities. However, even if the benefits of using technology for teaching may be clear, the cost is not. Costs tend to be under- rather than overestimated in this area, and management would be prudent to realize that the decision to make significant use of technology in teaching will almost certainly have to be accompanied by some very difficult decisions regarding funding reallocation and unit closures.

A third option is probably preferred, and that is to change the way we teach by replacing some face-to-face activities with technology-based learning and by making more effective use of faculty with the help of technology. For instance, by using Web-based materials, on-line group discussions, and e-mail, classroom teaching activities may be reduced by up to half, freeing the instructors for work on technology-based learning. Core teaching materials may be created that can be adapted for a variety of different courses or programs, thus reducing the number of instructors needed for new programs. Materials that are developed for on-campus students can be modified and adapted for continuing professional education, thus generating more revenues. In the end, a combination of strategies for reallocation and reorganization is likely to be necessary.

The biggest problem with reallocation as a strategy is that in their self-interest, faculty members will inevitably strongly oppose any moves to cut academic positions in order to fund the use of technology for teaching. Indeed, this can be avoided only if an institution continues to expand its activities and the number and range of students served, thus using technology to increase efficiency rather than to reduce existing jobs. For many institutions, doing more with the same or less resources is just the challenge they are facing, and thus a major reason why management looks to the use of technology.

Centralizing or Decentralizing Resources for Technology-Based Teaching

We have seen that in many of the strategies proposed, one fundamental issue is the degree to which decision making should be centralized and the degree to which it should be decentralized. Nowhere is this more critical than in funding reallocations. Should the senior management hold back a percentage of general purpose operating funds to finance the use of technology for teaching, or should it leave it to the deans and heads of department to make this decision?

Ideally, all departments and individual faculty would have a clear and shared vision for where technology fits into the teaching of the institution, and consequently would make rational and appropriate decisions about how funds should be spent. In this scenario, the more resources that can be devolved to departments the better. However, few institutions have managed to get themselves into this happy position. Until nirvana is reached, some alternative strategies are needed.

There are several factors to take into consideration. One is the issue of readiness and commitment. To what extent are the deans, heads of department, or individual faculty members committed to the innovative use of technology? Resources should flow to those who are willing and able to make use of the resources for the purposes for which they are intended.

Second, to what extent can deans, heads of department, or individual faculty members be trusted to use resources for teaching with technology rather than for other purposes, such as research, or keeping teaching programs going that would otherwise collapse? Asking this question does not imply that people are dishonest, but it recognizes the very real conflict of priorities that they face. If pressures are very strong to use resources for other purposes but the senior management really believes that using technology for teaching is a higher priority, then a central fund may be necessary.

Funding decisions also need to take into account the requirements of project management. One way to develop project management practices and skills is to use a central fund to fund projects and make the funding conditional on project management being implemented and followed. As experience grows, funds for project management can be pushed down to the faculty and departmental level.

Another issue is the availability and extent of technological infrastructure and specialist support for faculty members wishing to use technology for teaching. Institutions that already have good infrastructure and specialist support can afford to devolve to faculties and departments resources and decisions about how those resources should be used. If that infrastructure and support are not in place, then central management may need to give this a higher priority than devolving resources to faculties.

Central funding is a useful strategy for moving conservative faculties or departments into technology-based teaching and learning. However, once the majority of departments are committed to this, then resources for projects should be found within the normal faculty or departmental budget process.

I will return to the issue of decentralization in Chapter Eight. However, with respect to funding, it is likely that a mix of both centralized and decentralized approaches will be necessary.

Balancing Funding Between Infrastructure, Administrative Applications, and Educational Applications

In a context where resources are finite, you need to look at the total picture. Nowhere is this more important than in the balance between expenditure in technology infrastructure, administrative applications, and applications for teaching and learning purposes.

Because investment in infrastructure and administrative information technology systems has tended to precede investment in educational applications, it may be worthwhile in many institutions to take an audit of relative spending in these three areas and compare that with their "fitness for purpose." In some institutions, it may be time to slow down investment in further improvements to the technology infrastructure or administrative systems and reallocate at least some of the resources historically devoted to these other areas into educational applications. Increases in capital expenditure will usually need to be accompanied by increases in operating expenditure or the capital expenditure will be wasted. This means having a good understanding of the relationship between capital and operating expenditures, and working very closely with government officials and other funding agencies to ensure that budget allocations are in synch. Alternatively, if priorities for classroom teaching have historically dominated budget allocations, it may be time to switch resources into technical support for faculty.

These approaches, however, require a management structure that enables such cross-divisional and often cross-budgetary transfers or changes to be made. For instance, it may be necessary to transfer some funds out of one budget, such as the vice president of administration's, into another, such as the provost's, as priorities between infrastructure investment and educational applications change. Certainly, moving funding out of one budget holder's area into another's will be very difficult unless vision and strategies for technology have been agreed on by the management. I will return to this issue when discussing appropriate management organizational structures in Chapter Eight.

Developing Partnerships or Consortia

Technology-based distributed learning allows for courses developed in one institution to be available at another. Technology such as videoconferencing and the Internet can be used not only to deliver the courses from one institution to another but also for administrative and course team meetings between both institutions, whatever the distance.

Partnerships and consortia may be set up for a variety of reasons, but two of the most important are to share costs (or spread the same cost over greater numbers of students) and fight off perceived competition for students from other sources.

Partnerships Between Higher Education Institutions

The simplest arrangement is a partnership between two higher education institutions. Many universities have "memoranda of understanding" with many other universities, especially in foreign countries, which range from a vague statement of good will and intent to highly specific contractual arrangements. The purpose of the partnership may just be to exchange common experiences and learn from each other. It may be to facilitate exchange of students and staff, or to conduct joint research. It may be to share courses and to avoid duplication. It may be to share the cost of joint course development and delivery. And it may be to reach wider markets than each could have reached on its own.

Many state systems already have provision for transfer between colleges and universities. Students qualifying from a two-year college may transfer into the third year of a university program. This is much enhanced through technology-based distributed learning because the students may be able to take the third- and fourth-year courses at a distance, without moving from their community.

However, technology-based distributed learning opens up the possibilities of much more interesting partnerships. UBC's partnership with Monterrey Tech for five courses on technology-based distributed learning is based on a *franchise* arrangement. Monterrey Tech contracted with UBC to develop the courses, which could be laddered into Monterrey Tech's own Master's in Educational Technology and delivered electronically to its students at twenty-six campuses across Mexico as well as to several campuses in other Latin American countries. UBC also wanted to offer the courses to its own on-campus master's students and to noncredit students.

UBC developed the courses; Monterrey Tech paid for half the development costs. For this, Monterrey Tech obtained the rights to offer the courses in Latin America, and UBC retained the rights to offer the courses in the rest of the world. These courses are franchised because Monterrey Tech is responsible for marketing, recruiting, tutoring, and accrediting its own students. It can also enter into other agreements with other Latin American institutions to market these courses. Thus, it now has an agreement with Simon Rodriguez Experimental University in Venezuela to offer these courses.

Franchising has a number of advantages. The risk of developing technology-based courses is halved if a partner is willing to cover half the development costs. By franchising a course, difficult issues of admission and language prerequisites are avoided by the institution developing the courses. Having a local partner in another country provides local support services, such as counseling and tutoring. Having local tutors enables cultural and language issues to be addressed (some of Monterrey Tech's discussion forums are in Spanish, others are in English). The franchised institution has access to academic resources that would not otherwise be available and can draw on those resources for training of its own tutors, as well as for the students.

A franchise also enables far greater numbers of students to be handled. UBC is responsible for up to one hundred students per course. Monterrey Tech may have almost three hundred per course, but UBC does not have to worry about that; it is Monterrey Tech's challenge.

Last, through the partnership arrangement and the multiple use of the same materials for multiple target groups, these courses pay for themselves from fees from both UBC and Monterrey Tech students (see Bartolic and Bates, 1999, for full cost details).

There are many different possible variations on franchise arrangements. For instance, a third institution in another region, for example, the United States, could pay a "head tax" for every student enrolled at the originating institution and retain the remaining fee income after payment of its own costs, such as marketing, tutoring, assignment marking, and examinations. The third institution would thus avoid the high cost of development but still retain academic control over accreditation and student academic standards.

In a franchise arrangement, one institution develops a program and then another delivers it. Where several institutions are roughly equal in status, another partnership arrangement is for the *transfer of courses and credits* between institutions. Thus, several institutions may agree to develop a joint master's in sustainable resource management, as in the SEARCA example given in Chapter One. The partnering institutions would agree to an overall program curriculum, usually as a set of courses, then decide which of the partner institutions would develop *and* deliver different courses in the same program. These courses would be developed at least in a distributed learning mode but may also be available on campus as regular classroom courses.

Students in one institution would then be able to take courses offered by their own and other institutions and complete a full degree through a combination of courses from all the institutions. They could take courses from their own institution either in regular face-to-face classes (if available) or in distributed learning format while taking courses from the other institution at a distance. In some cases, students might "mix and match" distance and face-to-face courses at different institutions, if they can afford to travel.

Each institution would be responsible for its own courses, and credits would automatically transfer between them. A course may be entirely developed by one institution, but the others may appoint faculty members to review or provide feedback to ensure that the course from the other institution meets their own needs and standards.

The development cost, if course development is split equally, is slightly higher than proportionate to the number of institutions in the partnership developing courses. Thus if there are three partners, each institution may develop just one-third of a master's curriculum, but costs will be higher than one-third because of the need to review and approve courses from the other institutions. Also, one institution may wish to develop more than a third of the program, to give students more choice or to ensure that its specific needs are met.

In this arrangement, each institution retains the right to approve or reject the other's courses. The arrangement works best when partner institutions are of roughly the same status and have complementary strengths, that is, different areas of research or subject expertise that complement the other's. The main advantage besides cost is that students are able to access a wider range of expertise than would have been possible if restricted to their own institution's offering.

As well as franchise and credit transfer, partnerships can be developed through *joint course production*. In this arrangement, a team of academics from both institutions develops each course and the courses are jointly offered and accredited by each institution. Cleveland State University and Akron University have mounted a joint Master's in Social Work delivered by videoconferencing, with teaching shared between the two campuses.

Such courses can vary in the degree of integration. A thirteen-week, one-semester course might be divided into independent modules with different modules being developed and taught by faculty from different institutions. Ideally, the whole course is developed in an integrated manner by academics from both institutions working together as part of a team.

Students from both institutions would thus take the same course, and even the delivery might be done on a team basis, with tutoring being done by faculty from both institutions. Students from each institution may be randomly divided among tutors from each institution, regardless of the institution at which they are registered. They would take the same examination, and assessment would be divided between the academics from both institutions. If a whole degree program was developed this way, the degree might be awarded independently by the institution with which the student initially registered, or it might be a joint degree from both universities.

This is probably the most difficult model of partnership to pull off, but the most satisfying academically. If it works, the academics working together from different institutions are likely to develop a much richer and more challenging course than if they were working independently. However, it needs academics from both institutions who like and respect one another, and it is much more time consuming to develop such a course. Therefore, the savings, if any, are less than for a course independently produced.

Strategic Alliances

Sometimes used as a grand name for a partnership, a strategic alliance should really be used to denote a partnership between two or more organizations that has a long-term and strategic purpose, ideally resulting in something more than the sum of the two parts. UBC and Monterrey Institute of Technology in Mexico have a strategic alliance that includes the exchange of students and professors and the joint development of programs in several different content areas. The alliance is also aimed at enabling Monterrey Tech to access Asian markets more easily through UBC's Asian connections and at enabling UBC to access more easily Latin American markets through Monterrey Tech's connections.

A broad alliance provides a framework for individual initiatives within the alliance, such as the franchise arrangement for the distance education courses.

Consortia

Consortia involve more than two institutions in a collaborative arrangement. Consortia are nothing new in distance education. The three research universities and the Open Learning Agency (OLA) in British Columbia have operated a very successful consortium since 1979.

There are a number of elements to this consortium:

- An open access program enabling students to complete a full degree at a distance.
- They can do this by combining courses from the different universities and OLA, regardless of prior qualifications, or by transferring approved two-year college programs (usually taken in the conventional manner) into a two-year third- and fourth-year university degree program taken at a distance.
- Students who complete a degree this way are awarded a degree from the Open University of British Columbia through the Open Learning Agency, and the degree is recognized by government and the Association of Universities and Colleges of Canada. There have been over eleven hundred degree graduates through this program.
- Students can also transfer credits from one institution to another, so that a UBC student can take, for example, a distance education course from the University of Victoria and transfer it into his or her own UBC program.
- There is joint planning to avoid duplication of courses. The universities and OLA meet on a regular basis to exchange program information and to avoid duplication of distance education programs as far as possible. This operates on a voluntary basis.
- There is joint publicity and marketing of distance education courses and programs at a university level. OLA publishes a single calendar that lists all the courses and programs available by distance in the province at a university level.

- OLA also provides free student counseling and advisory services for anyone wanting to take a university-level distance education course.
- OLA operates a "credit bank," whereby students with qualifications from outside the province can have these accredited for use in the province, enabling them to transfer these credits into other partner institutions' programs.

The system has worked for so long and so well for three reasons. First, government funding is based on a fixed amount per full-time equivalent enrollment. Regardless of where the student finally graduates or even registers, the institution offering a particular course gets the equivalent FTE funding for each course enrollment.

Second, until recently the government put a small amount of money each year ($500,000 Canadian) into the consortium. Most of this was used for course development by the three universities, and the rest for the course calendar and student advice in distance education programs. Although the $500,000 was only a small proportion of what each institution put into distance education, it brought people to the table.

This funding has now been withdrawn, but the universities and OLA have agreed to continue the arrangements. Thus, the third reason why the system has worked is the willingness of the institutional leadership consistently to work collaboratively rather than in competition with each other in the province; this is perhaps the most unusual and important feature of the consortium.

The Western Governors' University is another form of consortium. It opened officially in June 1998. At the time of writing (April 1999) it had governors from eighteen member states, two Pacific territories, and a commonwealth as board members. It had twelve leading business partners, including Apple Computer, AT&T, Cisco, IBM, KPMG, Microsoft, Novell, and Sun. It had thirty-five participating educational institutions, including well-known state universities and colleges, such as the University of Wisconsin, Montana State, and Texas Tech.

WGU was created because of the founding governors' frustration that universities and colleges were not responding to the needs of business and industry and were not preparing students properly for the new world of work. It is based on the concept of *competency-based learning,* and the business partners are important because they help to determine the competencies required. WGU has no faculty, it does not plan to develop its own courses, and it has thrown out the concept of credit hours or "time spent" studying. Students can achieve their qualifications in two ways. The most innovative is by demonstrating set standards of competency through successful completion of tests and assessment, regardless of prior courses taken. Students will be advised, though, on how to reach these competencies through a personalized "academic action plan" (AAP). According to the WGU Web site (http://www.wgu.edu), an AAP is "developed by a WGU adviser-mentor in consultation with the student. The AAP will serve as a kind of a road map—complete with time lines and suggested learning activities—to guide the student through his or her entire academic program, while providing some valuable progress benchmarks."

WGU's "recognized" courses that produce the requisite competencies will be delivered by distance and will come from other providers, such as universities, colleges, and the private sector WGU will "broker" and validate these courses. (Go to http://www.wgu.edu/wgu/about/index.html for more information.)

In many ways, WGU is very similar to the Open University consortium in British Columbia, except on a much larger geographical basis (indeed, it has a partnership agreement with OLA). It has got off to a somewhat slow and controversial start, with, at the time of writing, low student enrollments, although there are over 100 courses in the catalogue and a projected 270 courses by September 1999. This still makes it smaller than the Open University of British Columbia consortium, which has had over 500 courses in its catalogue for the last ten years.

WGU's slow start is probably the result of a number of factors:

- Students need to see complete degree or credit programs, rather than individual courses, which complement or add to what they can obtain at a distance from their local and better-known institutions.
- It is always difficult to sell a new idea such as competency-based assessment when the rest of the system operates on a different and long-established basis of accreditation (no matter what its current limitations).

- Developing appropriate competency-based assessment is of it-self difficult and controversial at a higher education level.
- Providing individualized academic action plans is a labor-intensive and highly skilled activity and depends on a very wide range of resources being available to students.
- WGU probably needs more investment than it has received to date if it is to make a big impact; experience from the Open University in the United Kingdom and other nationwide open universities indicate that costs are almost always initially grossly underestimated.
- Finally, WGU is still dependent on mainline state institutions to provide the courses needed, and these institutions them-selves are often hostile to the concept, even if their governors support it. Students approaching conventional institutions then are likely to be directed to their own programs rather than the WGU's.

Although the Western Governors' University seems to be ini-tially struggling, it is probably too early to rush to judgment.

The Southern Regional Electronic Campus describes itself as a *marketplace* for on-line college courses across sixteen southern U.S. states. Students can identify programs and courses that are available electronically; search by college or university, discipline, level and state for more detailed information, including course de-scriptions and how the programs and courses are delivered; and connect directly to the college or university to learn about regis-tration, enrollment, and cost. However, there are currently no credit transfer arrangements and students still have to enroll di-rectly with a particular institution offering a course (go to http://www.srec.sreb.org/).

The California Virtual University is somewhat similar in oper-ation to the SREC. (California, with over 2.2 million adult learn-ers, and over 600,000 enrolled in its college and university system, opted out of WGU.) In November 1998 the CVU had 1,740 courses listed from 105 institutions and 11,000 enrollments. But the California Virtual University seems to be in even more trou-ble than WGU. It does not offer qualifications itself, and it does not arrange transfer of credit. Students still have to register with each university or college from which they wish to take courses.

At the time of writing, from a student's perspective it was nothing more than a catalogue of courses and also seemed to be considerably undercapitalized.

We are also beginning to see the start of international consortia of public universities. Universitas 21 is a collection of twenty-one "tier-one" research universities from Australia, Canada, East Asia, the United Kingdom, and the United States that are considering collaboration in a number of ways. UBC, which is a member of Universitas 21, is working with two other members of the consortia, the universities of Melbourne and Queensland, to develop joint programs in agricultural sciences, which can be offered not only in each country but also across East Asia.

A number of lessons can be learned from the experiences of these different consortia arrangements. In particular, the strength of a consortium can be measured by answers to the following questions:

- Can a potential student take a whole program through the consortium without having to physically move between institutions?
- Can a student automatically or without too much trouble transfer credits and courses from one institution to another within the consortium?
- Does the consortium provide "one-stop shopping," namely, student services (advice, counseling, and tutoring), registration for any institution in the consortium, fee payment, at any single point?
- Do students have a much wider range of choice of courses, and at a better quality, resulting from the consortium's activities?
- Is there consistency in fees between courses and programs offered by the various consortium partners? In other words, can a student pay the same fee for the same kind of course, irrespective of which consortium partner it comes from?

As suggested earlier, for consortia to work the members really need to be of roughly the same status, so that there are no barriers to credit transfer, movement of students between member institutions, and acceptance of common academic standards between the member institutions.

Virtual Universities

What is a virtual university? Facetiously, there are three aspects of current virtual universities. They have virtually no courses, they have virtually no students, and they are virtually whatever you want it them be!

More seriously, a virtual university is an organization that delivers courses and accreditation to students electronically. That is the bottom line. Within that very broad definition, there are many different kinds of arrangement.

Most virtual universities are in fact nothing more than a catalogue of on-line courses from an otherwise conventional institution, or a collection of on-line courses from several different providers (for example, California Virtual University), although most are striving for more than that.

Partnerships or Consortia with Private Sector Organizations

Increasingly, universities and colleges are entering into "partnerships" with a single company or group of companies to provide technology services to a campus or campus network. IBM, for instance, has developed partnerships with a number of institutions to provide IBM ThinkPad laptop computers for students. The university or college gets a special "deal" from IBM, in the form of lower prices, enhanced services, and sometimes free consultancy, in return for IBM being a preferred provider in a defined area. Similar partnerships have been developed between universities and telecommunications companies.

Another kind of partnership is when a university or college contracts with a private sector company to provide on-line courses. Colorado's community college system contracted with Real Education (now called e-College) to get its courses on-line "within sixty days."

A third kind of partnership is when a private sector organization offering its own courses enters into an arrangement with a public sector organization to provide credit for the courses. This enables students to get their fees paid by their employers or to get tax breaks on their fees. Both Microsoft and Novell have such a partnership with Tucson's Pima County Community College.

Partnerships with private sector organizations can bring genuine benefits to an educational organization. However, there are many dangers as well. In many cases, private sector companies use the term partnership for what is nothing more than a special marketing arrangement. A company may supply students with laptop computers or supply the institution with telecommunications at a very favorable discount. In return, the institution may be required to buy the hardware or software specified by the supplier of the laptops or sign an agreement that will make the telecommunications supplier an exclusive or preferred carrier. There is a danger of being tied into a particular technology or software, or particular technology supplier, when technology is changing so rapidly. The price of getting out of a partnership may be much higher than the benefits of getting in.

Types of Partnership Arrangements

Within these partnerships and consortia for technology-based distributed learning, several different arrangements can be identified:

Joint Marketing and Publicity of On-Line Courses

This seems to be the most common arrangement between higher education institutions in the United States, making increasing use of the Web to provide easy access to course information from a range of colleges or universities.

Marketing of Technology Services

Private sector organizations often seem to think of partnership with an educational institution as a special marketing arrangement, giving some benefits or deals to the organization that are not generally available to other institutions. Although such an arrangement may be beneficial to a university or college, it seems to me to be stretching and devaluing the meaning of the word partnership.

Credit Transfer

This for me is the bottom line in a partnership between educational institutions. If students cannot transfer credits between institutions, there seems to be little benefit for the students in such a partnership.

Prior Learning Assessment

This is wider than credit transfer. It recognizes not only prior qualifications but also prior competencies and learning experiences. The Western Governors' University has hung its hat on this arrangement. The challenge, though, is to find ways to assess economically such competencies.

Franchising

We have seen that there are many advantages to franchising. It works particularly well when there is a perception that the two partners may not be of equal status, or put another way, senate will not agree that students from another university, or the courses offered by that university, are as good as theirs. Partnership is sometimes feared as a back door entry for underqualified students who will then "swamp" an institution. Franchising provides a fire wall against these concerns.

Joint Course and Program Planning

This depends and builds on credit transfer between institutions, and it is most likely to work in consortia or partnerships of equals.

Joint Course Development

This is the toughest to do, and the most satisfying. This arrangement is entirely dependent on academics from different institutions respecting one another and sharing the same philosophy and interests regarding the subject matter.

External Accreditation

This agreement enables a private sector organization (for instance, Microsoft, Novell, or Sylvan Learning Systems) without a formal higher education charter to gain formal academic accreditation for its programs for their participants.

It can be seen that although technological delivery opens up many opportunities for partnership, it also raises a whole set of policy and procedural issues for institutions that are not themselves technology-related. Technology-based teaching and learning requires that these issues be addressed.

Keys to Successful Partnerships

There are many potential advantages in partnerships based on using technology for teaching, but developing successful partnerships or consortia needs a good deal of effort and skill. Here are some lessons learned.

1. Ensure that the partners are the right ones. What advantages, extra resources, or skills can they bring that your institution lacks? What can you offer to them? Will there be general support in the rest of the organization for these particular institutions being partners? Are there potentially better partners who would be willing to collaborate?

2. To get a partnership going, especially if it involves long distances between partners, put in the time and up-front investment. Presidents flying to each other's institutions for a day or so may be necessary, but it is certainly not sufficient. People, especially faculty members who have to work together, need to get to know one another. Although eventually much of the planning and development can be done at a distance, some face-to-face meetings are needed to get started. For this reason, a partnership is not worth doing in a small way. It has to have ambition. So what *strategic* benefits will accrue to each partner from the partnership? And who in an institution will take the risk of the up-front investment, knowing that the failure rate for partnerships is high?

3. Realize that the collaboration needs to operate at two levels: short term and long term. In the short term, it is important to get one or two collaborative courses going at each partner institution so that issues can be identified and addressed and linkages can be formed at an operational level. A long-term plan needs to be developed so that lessons learned from one project can be carried over to later projects, and most important, so that a coherent set of programs from a learner's perspective can be developed.

Even for short-term initiatives, certain issues need to be decided collectively by the partner institutions:

What is the primary target group for this course or program? Full-time campus-based students (existing market)? People in the workforce requiring a first degree (new market)? Continuing professional education? All of these?

Where will the students be located? In the normal recruiting area of each institution? Throughout the state or country of each partner institution? Globally?

Where will the students access this course or program? On campus? At home or work? Through local centers? In particular, is the course or program being offered primarily to enrolled students on campus at the institutions or to a wider target group?

Are there similar programs available at a distance offered by other institutions?

What are the unique strengths of each partner institution in this program?

What added value will the joint course or program provide compared with (a) each institution offering its own program, and (b) other, similar programs available at a distance from other providers?

What is the likely number of enrollments in this course each year? Will they be sufficient to justify the expense?

How will it be marketed?

What prerequisites will learners need?

Who will work on this course (what faculty members, and other contributors, for example, instructional designers, project manager, and so forth), and how much working time will they need?

What will be the working relationship between the partner institutions for this course or program? Joint development? Development by one partner but feedback and academic approval from the others? Independent production by one on the basis of trust by the others?

How will this program be approved in each of the institutions? Will it have to go through senate? If so, who will take responsibility for the process, and what are the likely chances of this getting through?

What technologies will be used for delivery? Will this work for all partners?

How will the tutoring and student assessment be done, who will do this, and how will it be paid for?

With which institution will students be registered and who provides accreditation?

What will it cost (a) to develop and (b) to deliver this program, over four or five years? How will the costs be shared between the institutions?

How will the course or program be maintained, and who will be responsible for this?

How will the program be paid for? From general operating funds? Tuition fees? External grants?

What happens to any profits or revenues from sales?

Who owns copyright?

4. If the partner institutions both have equal and matching capacity for technology-based distance delivery, decisions will need to be made about the relative roles of each unit. If one or more of the partners does not have this capacity, several strategies can be employed:

• The technology and distance education capacity at those institutions that do not have it can be strengthened. This is expensive, may have major policy implications, and consequently may take time to get resolved.

• One institution can provide training for another institution to help develop local technology and distance education capacity for managing Web sites, student services, and so on. This system is less costly and less risky and can ensure technological and working compatibility, but it will still take time and cost money.

• One institution can be used as the off-campus development and delivery arm for all the partners. This is an advantage if one of the partners has a full development and delivery system, including project management, instructional designers, copyright clearance, shipping, Web servers and maintenance, student services, and tutor payment systems all in place. If production and delivery is located with this partner, courses and programs can be developed and delivered as a marginal cost exercise. It does not really matter where a Web site is located, and if courses have to be delivered in more than one country, it does not really matter where the site responsible for delivery is located.

Serious problems are likely to arise if the partner institutions have developed different technologies for delivery of their own programs. An institution committed to using videoconferencing will face major challenges if the partnership moves to Web delivery, and vice versa.

5. Deans and heads of departments from the partner institutions will need to meet on a regular basis, by video- or audioconferencing as well as through e-mail and listserves. These meetings will be needed to decide on:

- A plan for collaborative programs
- Priorities for programming
- Identification of resources for production
- Assignment of responsibilities to individual faculty members for developing and delivering courses
- Monitoring of progress on course development
- Troubleshooting of issues as they are identified

6. Collaborative projects should be set up and managed on a project management model, with a clear task, an agreed-on budget that includes cash, staff time and access to necessary facilities, a production schedule, and a deadline for the first offering of a course or program. The deans or heads of departments from the respective institutions will need to identify sources of resources, both internally and externally.

7. Partner institutions should establish a formal agreement to collaborate, which should be signed off by the presidents. This will help publicize and legitimize the initiative, both internally and externally. However, this is best done *after* rather than before the preceding steps have been taken.

Conclusions

Funding decisions are the most important strategy available for management wishing to move an institution into (or away from) technology-based teaching and learning. Funding arrangements in many universities and colleges often have a historical basis and reflect earlier ways of doing things. Furthermore, funding and power often go together; those with the biggest budgets tend to have the loudest voices in financial decision making.

Consequently, senior management needs to look very closely at how well current financial strategy and current decision-making powers match the rapidly changing environment. In particular, management should examine whether funds need to be moved around in order to support the use of technology for teaching and what may be the major obstacles to changes in budget allocations.

Second, a major test of commitment to the use of technology for teaching and learning is the extent to which an institution is willing to use its base operating budget to support such activities.

Third, it is worth remembering that the kind of people needed to support technology-based teaching and learning are highly skilled and in short supply, and there is a steep learning curve in using these new technologies for teaching. Therefore, an institution should endeavor to attract and retain good staff in these areas. This is best done through regular or permanent positions rather than short-term funding, and that requires allocation of funds on a regular and recurring basis.

Also, in developing a financial strategy for supporting technology-based teaching and learning, as much attention should be paid to the potential of increased revenue generation as to increased expenditure. Technology allows new markets to be opened up and new sources of revenues from sales, licensing, and franchising of materials and courses. Nevertheless, technology, including the human resources needed to support the technology, on balance is likely to cost more each year, certainly over the short term, and this needs to be factored into financial planning.

Partnerships and collaboration are useful strategies for sharing costs and bring with them a number of academic and student access benefits. However, it is important to be clear about the objectives of a partnership, and in particular what the potential benefits will be for all partners. Developing successful partnerships takes time and money. The biggest challenge in developing a successful partnership is in finding the right chemistry between academics who are going to work together. Without that chemistry, little is likely to happen.

Chapter Eight

Organizing for the Management of Educational Technologies

When it comes to organizational structures, the challenge is to develop a system that encourages teaching units to be innovative and able to respond quickly to changes in subject matter, student needs, and technology. At the same time, redundancy and conflicting standards and policies across the institution must be avoided.

Putting too much emphasis on formal organizational structures can be dangerous. Staff willing to work collaboratively will often work around or across organizational boundaries, and perfect organizational arrangements will not work if petty jealousies and conflicting ambitions get in the way.

There is sometimes a tendency for senior managers to begin with organizational "tinkering" to get technology initiatives going before implementing any other strategies. Form, however, should be driven by function, and I have deliberately left organizational structures as one of the last strategies to be considered.

Central Technology Support Units

New technologies such as the Web appear to be decentralized. The power is often (or appears to be) on the desktop. This provides considerable empowerment for the individual faculty member. However, we have seen that high-quality educational multimedia requires a range of specialist skills that go beyond the capability of any single individual. Furthermore, the appearance of decentralization in the new technologies is deceptive. In fact, they depend on agreed-upon standards and networks for communication and interoperation as well as on human and technical support infrastructures that require policymaking across the institution.

We saw in Chapter Three that developing high-quality multimedia learning materials and distributed learning requires highly skilled staff, such as interface and graphics designers, media producers, instructional designers, Web programmers, and project managers. These people are expensive and in scarce supply, and even a large department would find it difficult to justify their full-time employment. Such specialized staff need a central base, where they can draw on the expertise and experience of their colleagues. A central unit can ensure that quality standards are followed in the development of technology-based teaching and learning.

Some institutions, especially in Australia (for example, the University of Wollongong, and Griffith University), have integrated their professional development, distance education, and media services units into a single multimedia department.

The University of Calgary has recently established an organization called the Learning Commons, described as "a community of learners and a network of scholars," which combines faculty development, distance education, multimedia production, and undergraduate curriculum reform. Faculty can apply for "fellowships" in the form of grants to work with or within the Learning Commons to develop multimedia teaching. It has a board of governors, mainly composed of faculty members, students, and some Learning Commons staff. Its subcommittees include teaching development, curriculum development, learning enhancement, and communications. (Go to www.ucalgary.ca/commons/ for more details.)

The University of Alberta has established an Academic Technologies for Learning (ATL) unit that supports the use of technology in teaching and learning initiatives at the University of Alberta. ATL provides workstations and highly skilled support staff to work with faculty to help them develop multimedia learning materials through its production studio. It supports distance education programs and is responsible for faculty development, evaluation and research, and instructional design. (Go to http://www.atl.ualberta.ca/ for more details.)

The California State University system has set up the Center for Distributed Learning (CDL), which is based at Sonoma State campus but serves all the campuses of the state system. This model is a particularly interesting one because CDL does not really develop courses but rather Web-based multimedia modules that instructors can integrate into their own teaching and adapt to their own specific approaches to teaching. For instance, CDL is developing fifteen Web-based experimental simulations in biology ("biology labs on-line"), which allow students to enter data and predict and test outcomes.

Even more significant is the Center for Distributed Learning's development of MERLOT (Multimedia Educational Repository for Learning and Online Teaching), which is based around the idea of *learning objects*. To quote the group's Web site: "The Multimedia Repository Initiative will provide an opportunity for students and faculty to share, and find, valuable resources for learning and teaching. Faculty will be invited to identify any work they wish to make available to the educational community at large, and to post them in MERLOT. . . . Private collections of still images, video, and sounds will be archived and shared over the WWW. The repository will also provide a forum for the academic technical support staff of the CSU to share support strategies and find answers to technical questions." (Go to http://cdl.edu for more details on the work of the Center for Distributed Learning.)

In the future, we may see less and less development of whole courses by teams of specialists working with subject experts, and more and more development of small learning objects, from single diagrams to complex expert systems. Instructors and students will be able to download these learning objects and integrate them in their own teaching and learning programs or "virtual environments." The main barrier to greater development of learning objects is not so much technological as financial. A system of protecting rights and funding the development, storage, retrieval, and indexing of such learning objects needs to be put in place. The CDL experiment is an important first step.

The establishment of six cooperative multimedia centers in Australia, with university and business partners, suggests that multimedia production and services may even be shared among several neighboring universities and private sector organizations.

It can be seen that many organizations are struggling to find the most appropriate way of establishing a central support service.

Some are beginning to integrate what were previously separate units into one central unit. Note also that in some of the central units, such as the Learning Commons, technology-based teaching and learning is just part of a wider approach to teaching and learning.

Decentralized Services

There is a long history in universities and colleges of setting up large, central technology units. In the 1960s and 1970s many universities invested in expensive, centrally managed television studios. More recently, universities have established large, central computing organizations.

Too often, these central services have had little impact on the core teaching activities of an institution, partly because academics have felt that they had no control over them. Such units are often subjected to attempts by deans to break them up and reallocate their funding back to the faculties, especially if these central services have to operate on a cost-recovery system and therefore charge departments for their services.

An important study of managing technology for teaching and administration in Australian universities (Australian Graduate School of Management, 1996) classified universities into three different groups: old, divisional, and new. The study argued that although centralization of services is appropriate in a new institution with a major commitment to make IT a center of its vision and strategy, it is less likely to be appropriate for the old or well-established "divisional" universities with large and powerful faculties.

It is certainly true that at many universities and some colleges there are concerns not to weaken the control of faculties over the teaching process and to avoid setting up a large central unit that might develop its own autonomy. Consequently, many institutions (such as UBC) have so far not gathered all the different support services into one central unit. Instead, the organization retains several small-size organizational units with somewhat linked activities. Media Services may provide more traditional printing, photography, audio and video production, and videoconferencing facilities. Distance education may have instructional designers and desktop editors. A center for faculty development may have a focus on improving face-to-face teaching more than technology-based teaching. The campus computing organization may provide network services across campuses and technical support for multimedia production.

There is a risk that all these separate services will consider new technologies to be part of their mandate and will start duplicating services and competing for resources. In this context, individual faculty members or departments may start hiring graduate assistants to provide educational technology support, and may or may not call on one or other of the multiple support units for help. Some faculties or departments who are more advanced or more voluminous in their use of new technologies may establish their own "flexible learning" or multimedia units.

Multiple centers of activity is still the prevailing model in many universities and colleges. It is often a recipe for chaos, and it always results in massive duplication. There is no center of expertise in multimedia production, instructional design, or distributed learning, and no requirement for instructors to meet universitywide standards or use professional services.

A Lightly Coordinated Decentralized Model

In a mixed model of centralization and decentralization, there could be a small central unit, perhaps titled Center for Educational Technology. This unit will have a few highly specialized and skilled staff, such as a multimedia interface designer or graphics designer and an advanced Web specialist (without any specialists, such a center would lack credibility). The center will also have a director whose main job is to coordinate and facilitate collaboration between faculty members and support units, and to organize specialist support when needed. The other support units, such as media services, distance education, and campus computing, will still exist independently.

For large projects, teams can be called together from across the various groups and coordinated by the Center for Educational Technology. Thus, a project to develop an introductory microbiology course combining a CD-ROM with the Web may have a couple of faculty members and a project manager from the faculty of science, an instructional developer from health sciences, graphics and interface design from the educational technology center, media production from media services, and an Internet specialist from the distance education unit.

Figure 8.1 depicts the kind of arrangement just described.

Funding through a project management model will facilitate this kind of model, although it could also be paid for on a fee-for-service basis by the faculty or department if it is able to find funds for this purpose.

A Model Organizational Structure

Each of the preceding models has major weaknesses. With a decentralized approach, there is no professional center to provide standards and career support and development for support staff and no strategic or regular funding to support technology-based initiatives. With a centralized approach, there is insufficient support close to faculty members.

To overcome these limitations, and to provide support on a large enough scale to ensure that technology-based teaching and learning really has an impact on the work of an institution, a more ambitious and comprehensive model is required. This model is based on a fairly large professional center—perhaps titled the Uni-

**Figure 8.1. A Coordinated Decentralized Model
of Multimedia Design and Development.**

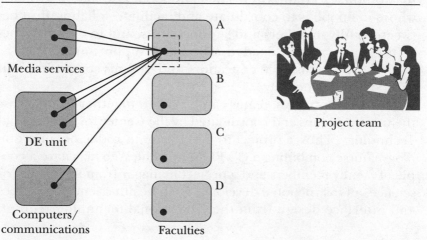

versity Teaching and Learning Center—offering an extensive range of university- or collegewide services combined with support for instructors at a local level.

The following model is based on a large research university with some thirty thousand students and assumes that about half the academic staff is engaged in extensive use of technology-based teaching, for on-campus or off-campus students. The model can be scaled up or down depending on the size of the institution and its commitment to the use of technology for teaching.

The target funding for the central unit would be approximately 2 percent of the overall teaching budget. The target funding for local or departmental support for instructors would be approximately 3 percent of the overall teaching budget, giving a total of 5 percent of the teaching budget devoted to academic technology support. (This is *in addition* to general technology support for a department or faculty provided by central computing services, for instance.)

In this model, each faculty or large department would have a small flexible learning unit, consisting of one technical support person for every twenty-five academic staff using technology for teaching and one generalist educational technologist for every fifty academic staff using technology. (This is somewhat similar to the Collège Boréal model.)

The technical support people would look after the technical construction and maintenance of Web sites, manage the teaching servers, ensure that multimedia software is properly installed and running, and help instructors to use it, and they would provide general computer support in the classroom or computer labs. These staff could be seconded from a central computing support service.

The general educational technologists, who may be graduates of the department in which they work, will have received some training in both instructional design and educational technology, probably from the central support unit. An educational technologist's main job would be to help identify technology-based projects in the department or faculty, provide immediate assistance for small-scale applications, and find appropriate support from the center for larger, more ambitious projects. These support staff would be funded by faculty or departmental funds, and a senior academic would be responsible for the unit on a part-time basis.

In addition to this departmental or faculty support, a central professional teaching and learning support center would have the following functions:

- Strategic planning assistance to teaching departments
- Project management in partnership with teaching departments
- Instructional design support
- Educational technology support (software selection, graphics, interface design, Web, and other Internet support services)
- Monitoring and dissemination of new developments in university teaching and educational technologies
- Faculty development, including the educational training of teaching assistants
- Videoconferencing support, video and audio production, digital compression facilities, CD-ROM production, Web server operation or support
- Multimedia training and development for faculty
- Research and evaluation of new teaching initiatives in the institution

This center would operate in the following way:

- It would be a support and service unit for faculties and teaching departments.
- It would work in partnership with teaching departments.
- Its priorities and directions would be established by an academic board.
- It would operate on a project management model, which would include management of project funds, staff, and facilities.
- Its projects would have clear "deliverables" in that the projects result in significant and sustained teaching activities of a different nature from that which existed before the project, by a set deadline.
- Each project should lead to more cost-effective use of resources over the long term.
- It would be established by a reallocation of funds and coordination of previously existing services and staff.
- New resources would be limited to filling critical skills gaps that were not already available elsewhere in the institution (for

example, interface design) before the establishment of the center.

- Many of its staff would be seconded to work in faculties on a continuing basis.
- It would provide a professional base for all teaching support staff, whether appointed by the center or by faculties or departments.
- It would gradually devolve its resources, services, and methods of operation to faculties.

The academic board would be a mix of an academic associate vice president or vice president (who would chair the board), one or two deans, academics from other faculties appointed by deans or elected by academic staff, student representatives, the director of the center, and one or two elected center staff. The board would allocate funds for approximately seventy-five to a hundred projects a year (around $500,000 a year).

The technology would be an important part, but only a part, of the work at the center. Its focus would be on supporting teaching and learning.

The center might have the following resources: a director; a manager of course production overseeing ten to fifteen project managers or instructional designers, most of whom will be working on projects or seconded to work in a particular faculty or department; a manager-producer of multimedia production overseeing one advanced Web specialist and one multimedia graphics designer, one interface designer, two media producers, and two technical support staff; two curriculum development specialists; two faculty development staff; two researchers (possibly externally funded); two administrators, one a general manager and one for special services who would supervise eight to ten administrative staff (mainly to provide student services for off-campus students); $500,000 to $1 million per annum in cash for new projects (including funds for buying out academics to work on projects); and $500,000 to $1 million operating funds. The total annual operating cost of the center would be in the order of $3 million to $5 million, including salaries and benefits.

In total, the cost of both central and local academic technology support could come to about $10 million per annum, or 5 percent of the total teaching budget in a large research university. The amount of $10 million may seem large, and indeed if it has to be found by reallocation of funds it *is* a large amount. However, many institutions are already paying this in distributed technical support services, hiring of graduate students, teaching improvement grants, faculty development, curriculum reform, external contracting, and distance education funding. (This center would provide support for both on-campus and distance learners.) If the *hidden* costs of academic staff doing their own technology support is factored in, the figure is probably much higher.

Again, I am not advocating that institutions *should* spend this much money on technology for teaching and learning. However, if an institution is committed to the extensive use of technology for teaching, for on-campus as well as off-campus students, this is likely to be the order of cost if it is to do it well.

Bureaucratic and Administrative Issues

The dominant organizational structure of most universities and colleges today is fairly hierarchical and strongly divisional. Senior managers (such as presidents, vice presidents, vice chancellors) are responsible for activities throughout the institute. Deans are responsible for separate collections of departments, each with their own head or chair. Instructors are ranked by seniority in the form of full professors, associate professors, senior lecturers and lecturers, assistant professors, sessional lecturers, and teaching assistants.

Some universities, such as the University of Sussex in Britain, have been more successful than others in organizing around interdisciplinary areas or themes. In general, this kind of university has been the exception rather than the rule. The main form of organization has been around subject disciplines, organized into divisional faculties.

The organizational structure of large universities and colleges still bears a strong resemblance to industrial (or Fordist) models of organization. This is despite the complicating factors of faculty dominance of senate, elected deans, limited terms of office for vice presidents, and so on, all of which tend to provide checks and balances for a hierarchical command model of decision making.

One particular feature of large universities and colleges is their bureaucracy, both in terms of policies and procedures, and the numbers of employees in administrative and support roles. Another common feature of larger higher educational institutions is the resistance by deans to centralization of academic resources and services. Faculties are often run as semiautonomous, almost baronial enterprises.

New technologies, however, work best in the postindustrial organizational style described in Chapter Two. The danger is that innovation and new initiatives will have to be managed and organized outside the traditional institutional bureaucracy and hierarchies if they are to be successful. Smith (1991), in a review of Canadian universities, noticed that innovation took place mainly at the periphery, in divisions such as continuing studies, and the funding for such innovations was usually from outside the general purpose operating fund of the institution. Thus, the core structure of the university is little changed by such innovations.

This is indeed a feature of the UBC–Monterrey Tech courses discussed earlier. They were self-funded and developed primarily as noncredit courses, and the master's component is still working its way through a raft of departmental, faculty, and senate committees for approval (seventeen committees in all). The process is expected to take two and a half or three years, by which time the whole program will have been delivered.

Establishing the necessary administrative support procedures for the UBC–Monterrey Tech courses was even more of a challenge. One problem was registering UBC graduate and certificate or noncredit students for the courses. UBC undergraduate credit students (including those taking distance education courses) normally register for courses through UBC's automated telephone registration service, Telereg. However, as this was the first graduate-level course to be offered as a distance education course at UBC, the Telereg system would not accept registration for these courses. (According to a policy decided over ten years ago by the western Canadian deans of graduate studies, graduate students were not to be allowed to take graduate courses at a distance. This policy has since been modified but the computer block on Telereg has not been removed.) Telereg cannot register certificate or noncredit students, either.

Therefore, forty UBC students had to register through the DE&T office. Establishing a new on-line system of registration in a very short time was a significant challenge, resolved internally by a DE&T administrator with database training. As a result, DE&T has now its own fully automated on-line registration system for distance graduate and noncredit courses, which allows students not only to register but also to order materials and pay electronically. (Go to http://itesm.cstudies.ubc.ca/info/ to see this system.)

Another serious organizational issue was the UBC bookstore's difficulties in dealing with distance students. The main problem was in their payment policy. The UBC bookstore requires that payment be received and cleared before materials can be delivered. However, international money orders can sometimes take up to a month to process. For instance, we had a student in Yugoslavia. She had to get her employer to pay first for the course, then for the materials. Then she had to purchase two international money orders and mail them to Canada. In the meantime, the student had to wait for the payment to be processed before the course materials were sent.

Furthermore, the UBC bookstore did not have a system set up for tracking orders that were shipped. The materials were sent to the international students once their payments were processed. However, after leaving UBC, there was no way of knowing what happened to the course materials, including whether the materials had been received by the students. In one case, the course materials sat at a customs office for over a month because the student was not notified of their dispatch.

In order to solve these problems, the Distance Education and Technology unit (DET) at UBC has now developed a "one-stop shopping" approach. Students can choose both to register and pay DET directly on-line for the course materials as well as the course in a single payment. DET orders the materials from the bookstore in advance of the course opening and then mails or sends them by messenger directly to the students when they register and pay. Students are informed by e-mail when the materials are dispatched

The UBC library receives special funds from the university to support UBC credit distance education students, through a service called the extension library. Registered credit students can order (on-line) up to thirty requests per course and the article or book will be mailed to the student, whatever the location. However, those enrolled as certificate or noncredit students do not receive the same service (unless they pay for a library card; UBC students receive free access). Consequently, UBC library is now piloting access to certificate and noncredit students on one of the subsequent courses, to identify the impact on cost and service.

It is important not to misunderstand the message here. UBC's academic staff and administrators are not stupid or incompetent. The systems have been developed for quite different circumstances from technology-delivered teaching. It is actually to the credit of UBC academic staff and administrators that when presented with a problem, they have been in general more than willing to suggest solutions and make the necessary changes. We are now in the process of trying to integrate these services developed in the Distance Education and Technology unit into the regular academic and administrative units.

The challenge, though, in a truly postindustrial university is for such new programs to be reviewed and approved quickly and efficiently in the normal operation of a department or faculty. The registration, financial, and other operational systems must be able to handle this type of program as part of their normal activities.

At the same time, previously central services, such as financial systems, the registry, and computers and communications, are being decentralized as information systems move away from large central mainframe information processing to a more distributed computer service based on local but networked server technology. This decentralization possibility for administrative systems, combined with the need for one-stop shopping and integrated services, could have a profound impact on the traditional division between faculties and administrative services, and even more so on the faculty divisional structure itself. It is likely to result in a move away from large, hierarchical, "vertical" divisions, to small, horizontal, integrated operations.

Because of the difficulties in making these changes in regular institutions, it could be argued that it would be more effective to set up a completely parallel organization for "nonconventional" programming, titled, for example, the Virtual University or Extension College. However, this runs the risk of conventional faculties and operational units being completely left behind by changes in the external environment to the point where they begin to become irrelevant or unattractive to "mainline" students. Also, a parallel system would lead to a great deal of unnecessary duplication.

However, some fundamental organizational changes may be required to ensure that new approaches and methods become part of the core activities of an institution. Strong discipline-based departments organized in a large division or faculty and dependent on a highly formalized system of course approval are major barriers to innovation and change, as are large, central administrative units.

In contrast, academic units might be organized into small, issue- or theme-related areas, with one or two of their own technology and administrative support staff in each unit, drawing on central or external specialist services as and when required. With the move to server technology, previously centralized areas such as registration and financial services could be largely decentralized to the theme-related academic units, with the central units being more concerned with coordination, training, innovation, and overall policy than with day-to-day operations. Still, so much is invested in the current way of doing things in such large units that it will need a major effort to change them.

Management Structures for Supporting Academic Technology

In the private sector a number of organizations have recognized the strategic importance of information technology by appointing a single chief information officer at the vice president level with full-time responsibility for information technology policy throughout the organization. This person is not necessarily someone who has come from a career in computing or communications, but rather often a staff person with expertise and experience in the area of business of the company who also has developed a good understanding of the issues of managing information technologies.

In contrast, many universities and colleges have a bicameral line management structure, with an academic vice president responsible for academic policies and one or more vice presidents responsible for administration. Usually the management of the institutional technology infrastructure reports through the vice president of administration or the vice president of student services.

The division of responsibilities between technology and academic activities is not necessarily an issue if senior management has the same vision for the direction of the institution, and in particular the role of technology in the institution; the vice presidents work collegially and collaboratively and get on well with one another; and there is a mechanism in place for bringing technology issues to the table for discussion by the whole senior management team. Virginia Tech is a good example of an institution with such a collegial management style. However, these conditions do not always prevail in the senior management of even well-run institutions, so a formal management structure that "fits" the needs of academic technology management can be valuable.

I do not believe that in a research university environment, a chief information officer can take responsibility for both academic and administrative technology, although I know of several colleges where this seems to work well, particularly if the CIO has come from an academic background. My preference is to have an associate vice president, academic, with overall responsibility for academic technology issues, probably as part of a larger remit for teaching and learning. But it will be critical for this person to work closely with the head of computing and telecommunications services.

Even with line management responsibilities clarified, there is still probably a need for structures for setting and coordinating information technology policy at an institutional level. This should include those responsible for technology infrastructure, academic technology policy, and administrative requirements. If technology plays a significant part in the teaching of the university or college, one of the vice presidents (probably the provost) should chair such a committee.

It will also be critical for the academic vice president to have an academic technology advisory committee in place. This should include:

- Representative faculty members, some of whom should have extensive experience in using technology for teaching.
- A dean or two.
- The director of the teaching and learning center.
- The librarian.
- The person responsible for the technology infrastructure. (This could be the same academic board controlling the university teaching and learning center proposed earlier.)

Whatever the advantages and disadvantages of these various arrangements, what is needed is a set of mechanisms by which institutionwide policies and priorities for information technology can be determined and implemented. These mechanisms should ensure that academic technology concerns are appropriately represented and addressed.

Conclusions

I have argued that a mix of centralized and decentralized technology support services is required. No single academic department or even large faculty can afford to employ the whole range of specialized support staff required for the development of high-quality technology-based courses. However, these central units should cover a wider range of activities than just academic technology support, such as curriculum development, faculty development, instructional design, project management, research and evaluation of institutional teaching and learning, and advanced multimedia production facilities.

The danger of such central units is that they in turn would become too large to manage efficiently, be seen as diverting resources from core academic activities (especially by those opposed to the use of technology for teaching), or remain outside the main academic teaching stream. This can be tempered by seconding specialist academic technology staff from the central unit to work for short periods in academic units, for academic units to have their own generalist support staff, or by seconding faculty members for short periods to work in the center. Another solution might be to retain smaller, separate central specialist units, and use project management models to bring them together for specific purposes on an as-needed basis.

Nearly all higher education institutions are currently underfunding technical and instructional support for technology-based teaching. I have argued that if an institution is really committed to using technology for teaching, it needs to devote at least 5 percent of its overall teaching budget to such support.

Using technology to extend the campus on a global basis will affect all aspects of a university or college, but particularly administrative systems. New server technology not only allows technology to be used for teaching but also administrative systems to be more decentralized. Both administrative systems and academic policies will need to be under constant review as distributed learning begins to spread throughout the institution. Academic policies and administrative procedures developed for another age and environment will remain major barriers to the use of technology for teaching.

Information technology now is a core, mission-critical area for all universities and colleges, and it includes academic as well as administrative needs. Consequently, the use of information technologies needs to be coordinated, and policy and investment needs to be planned at the most senior institutional management level.

New forms of academic and administrative organization are likely to be needed to support new types of courses, new types of learners, and new learning needs, whether or not technology is used. It may require the radical restructuring of faculties, academic departments, and central administrative units to do this. The alternative is to develop completely parallel systems to "protect" traditional units, which in turn may lead to internal competition, fragmentation, and duplication of services.

In a number of private sector organizations, a single chief information officer has been appointed at a senior level to develop policy and coordinate all activities requiring the processing of information and use of technology. However, the CIO model appears to be difficult to operate at least in large universities, given the traditional division of academic and administrative responsibilities.

The impact of new technologies and the pressures that they are placing on current organizational structures are only slowly being recognized. Thus, the radical changes suggested here may not be necessary. It may be possible through relatively minor structural changes in organization to accommodate the needs of new technologies. However, evidence from institutions such as Collège Boréal, Virginia Tech, and Sonoma State, where technology is being fully integrated into all teaching and learning activities, indicates that the intensive use of technology for teaching does seem to require radical changes in organizational structure to support its use.

Chapter Nine

Research and Evaluation

At the time of my writing this book, no conventional campus-based higher education institution has had extensive experience in using the Internet and multimedia in a sustained and intensive manner for teaching purposes. This means that successful and sustainable planning and management strategies have yet to be clearly identified and documented.

Given the rapid speed with which new technologies for teaching are infiltrating even the most cautious and conservative of universities, and the lack of experience in the use and management of such technologies, the case for researching and evaluating the applications of these new technologies is obvious.

Such research and evaluation, though, needs to be focused on the right questions, and it needs to be done in ways that help inform planning and management decisions. In other words: What seems to work and what doesn't in planning and managing new technologies for teaching and learning?

Evaluating Teaching and Learning Through New Technologies

The place where most faculty members and graduate students tend to start is by evaluating the relative effectiveness of technology-based teaching compared with traditional face-to-face teaching. Although this may be necessary to win buy-in from reluctant faculty members, this particular research agenda is frankly a waste of time. The results are already known.

Asking the Right Questions

There have been many thousands of well-conducted research studies comparing a televised lecture, or computer-based learning, or print-based correspondence education, or any of a range of other technologies, with classroom lectures. Furthermore, there has been a remarkable consistency of results dating back from the early 1970s: the most common finding from all the carefully conducted research with well-balanced comparative groups, objective learning measurements, and large enough samples is that there is no significant difference in student performance.

The generally accepted conclusions from all these studies is that teaching with technology does at least as well, if not better, as conventional classroom teaching (see, for instance, Schramm, 1974; Clark, 1983; Moore and Thompson, 1990; Russell, 1999).

It is often further inferred from the no-significant-difference results that in the end, it does not really matter what technologies are used for teaching because there is "no significant difference" between their use and classroom teaching. This, however, is a false inference, because the research design has usually deliberately excluded other factors than the original classroom learning objectives. These other factors may be the crucial deciding factors that make it worthwhile to use a particular technology or not.

There are several reasons for the no-significant-difference results. The first is that the traditional classroom is nearly always used as the basis for comparison. In other words, can the new technology achieve the *same objectives* as those sought in the classroom? Very often, the same teaching method (for example, didactic lecture) is then applied to the new technology. Indeed, quantitative researchers such as Clark (1983) insist that for experimental reasons, all other conditions *except* the choice of technology or teaching medium must remain the same for a true scientific comparison to be made.

The problem with this kind of research is that very often, *different* or new learning outcomes can best be achieved through the use of technology. For instance, a didactic lecture may be concerned primarily with content acquisition and comprehension, whereas a Web-based course may be more concerned with students seeking, analyzing, and evaluating information. Restricting technology merely to imitating the assumptions and goals of classroom teaching in order to assess scientifically its comparative worth is like cutting two legs off a horse to see if it can run as fast as a man.

Thus, although straight comparisons of face-to-face teaching with technology-based teaching are not very helpful, research into the unique contributions that technology can make to teaching and learning is. Such research would focus on the relationship between the use of a technology and different levels or types of learning (see Laurillard, 1995, for a fuller discussion of this).

Another problem with straight, quantitative, comparative research is that there are usually greater differences in learning outcomes *within* a particular technology or medium of teaching than *between* them. Thus, a good lecture will always have better learning outcomes than a poorly designed multimedia program, *and vice versa*. One important lesson from this is that good technology does not save bad teaching. It not only makes it worse but also spreads it more widely. However, research that focuses on the requirements for the effective use of a particular technology will be helpful. Such research might focus on forms and levels of student-machine interaction, interface design, and designs that support learners working in isolation.

Teachers, learners, and technologies are all amazingly flexible in their abilities to teach and learn. If one technology is not available to a teacher, then she may get just as good results using another approach, although there will be other losses (and some gains), such as the teacher spending more time or the student having to work harder. These "side effects" are often the truly important benefits (or limitations) of using new technologies, but they are usually excluded by comparative research design.

In developing strategies for research and evaluation, we need to look at a wider range of factors than the ability of technology to replicate classroom teaching. The ACTIONS model following indicates some of these factors.

The ACTIONS Model

In an earlier publication (Bates, 1995), I identified the following factors that need to be considered when evaluating the effectiveness of different teaching technologies. These factors may be summarized by the acronym ACTIONS:

*A*ccess and flexibility: How accessible is a particular technology for learners? How flexible is it for a particular target group?

*C*osts: What is the cost structure of each technology? What is the unit cost per learner? How do costs differ between technologies within a particular context?

*T*eaching and learning: What kinds of learning are needed? What instructional approaches will best meet these needs? What are the best technologies for supporting this teaching and learning?

*I*nteractivity and user-friendliness: What kind of student interaction does this technology enable? How easy is the technology to use?

*O*rganizational issues: What are the organizational requirements, and the barriers to be removed, before this technology can be used successfully? What changes in organization need to be made?

*N*ovelty: How new is this technology? How reliable is it? How will this technology contribute to institutional renewal?

*S*peed: How quickly can courses be mounted with this technology? How quickly can materials be changed?

Thus, new technologies for teaching do need to be researched and evaluated, but the evaluation should not be restricted merely to replicating classroom learning outcomes. Research and evaluation questions that are more relevant might include these:

• *What impact will this application of technology have on student access and flexibility to learn?* Will this enable new markets to be reached or new needs to be served, or will this technology disadvantage learners that we currently serve?

• *What are the cost advantages and disadvantages of applying this technology?* What will be the impact on costs of increasing student numbers this way compared with increasing student numbers through traditional classroom teaching? What happens to costs if student enrollments drop? At what point in terms of student numbers does this technology become more cost-effective than other approaches?

- *What teaching functions and learning outcomes seem to be more easily or more effectively achieved through the use of this technology?* What learning objectives appear difficult to achieve using this technology? Will this technology enable us to achieve learning objectives previously not considered, and are these outcomes worthwhile?

- *What forms and levels of interaction can be achieved in using this technology?* Does it give reliable and comprehensive feedback to students? Can students ask open-ended questions and receive prompt responses? Does the technology encourage or facilitate discussion between students? What kind of thinking—comprehension, analysis, problem solving, decision making, or evaluation—does this technology encourage? Is the technology easy to use by learners and teachers?

- *How easy is the technology to operate and manage?* Is the necessary infrastructure already in place or does it need to be built? Does the institution have sufficient technical, production, and educational staff available to support this technology? If not, can they be found locally at reasonable cost? Is the technology demanding of technical support time? Does it require a lot of help to be provided to students? Will the administrative systems have to be changed to accommodate the planned uses of this technology?

- *How reliable and stable is the technology?* Has it been thoroughly tested before being made available to students? How much training is needed both for teachers and learners before this technology can be used effectively? To what extent is the department or institution prepared to support new initiatives in this area?

- *How quickly can courses be mounted or materials developed using this technology?* How quickly and easily can changes be made or new material added? How quickly and easily can the materials be distributed to learners?

These questions provide a basis for the selection of technologies and their subsequent evaluation. (For more details on selecting and using new technologies for teaching and learning in higher education, see Bates, 1995.)

Researching Software Applications

The choice of appropriate software to support the development of technology-based courses (course authoring software) is a complex issue for several reasons. There is a wide range of course authoring products available, new products appear on the market all the time, and existing products may be substantially improved in later versions. In addition, course developers need to be aware of general software developments that can dramatically affect technology-based teaching, such as learning objects (see Chapter Eight for more on learning objects), new languages such as Java, video servers, screen sharing, and search engines. Merely keeping up to date with software developments is a full-time job.

For these reasons, there is an understandable tendency to shy away from doing the research necessary to identify the "best" software solution. Consequently, "Paulian conversion" is a common form of decision making: an administrator or professor attends a conference or trade exhibition, sees a particular technology, and is immediately "converted" in the same manner as was St. Paul on the road to Damascus. Thereafter, all course development must be forced into this particular technology.

Some institutions have tried to standardize on one course authoring system in order to keep down administrative costs. This is a major decision, one that will have implications for all instructors wanting to develop technology-based courses. The drawback to standardizing on a particular type of course development software is that there are many different ways in which one can teach, and no software yet exists that suits all purposes. For instance, the software needed to develop a Web-based course with a heavy emphasis on classroom discussion will be very different from the software needed to develop a multimedia CD-ROM based on an expert system for decision making. Even in courses totally confined to Web delivery, a wide range of teaching approaches is possible, depending on the nature of the subject matter and the preferred teaching approach of the faculty member.

Thus, any attempt to impose a single course authoring software solution on a whole institution is likely to impose a serious restriction on academic freedom and could lead to a highly undesirable uniform approach to teaching across all subjects. It is particularly important that administrators or computer systems managers do not make such decisions without full prior discussion with faculty members.

It is not surprising that research into different Web authoring software, such as WebCT, Lotus Notes Learning Space, and so forth, for supporting technology-based teaching, is seen as an essential activity, and indeed it is. Several Web sites provide comparative analyses of different Web-based course authoring software (see, for instance, http://www.ctt.bc.ca/landonline/; http://sunil.umd.edu/webct/; http://www.umanitoba.ca/ip/tools/courseware/). The problem is that these Web sites generally focus on technical issues (reliability, speed, server requirements, and so forth) and sometimes also on administrative and cost issues. Although it is necessary to consider such factors, they are not sufficient for teaching and learning purposes. Research should be focused just as much on the compatibility of different software with different teaching approaches as on administrative and cost factors.

The complexity of such decisions also argues for a central academic unit with special expertise that can track new developments in software and their applicability to teaching and learning, and can act as a guide and educator for faculty members on software developments.

Although evaluation of appropriate course authoring software should be an ongoing activity, it is only one of many other important factors that can influence the success or otherwise of technology-based courses. Indeed, there are many examples of technology-based courses that have been successful despite poor decisions being made on appropriate software. In other words, software evaluation should not be the sole or even main priority for research.

Learner Impact

In addition to measuring learning outcomes, it is important to assess the other effects on learners of technology-based teaching. One of the great challenges facing traditional campus-based institutions will be getting the balance right between face-to-face and technology-based teaching, particularly for young freshmen coming direct from high schools. Also, with increasing emphasis on lifelong learning, widening access, continuing professional education, and applied graduate programs, the demographics of the student body are likely to change. It will be important to track learners' responses to a shift in teaching methods and to identify any differences in response by the type of student.

For students, there is often a trade-off between loss of direct, personal contact and increased access and flexibility. There is also a trade-off between the costs of getting to campus and the costs of acquiring a computer, software, and Internet access. Response again is likely to vary with demographics. My experience suggests that technology-based learning is more acceptable and more affordable to working adults. Young freshmen on campus tend to prefer more conventional forms of teaching and need to be eased gently into learning via technology, because it requires more self-discipline and personal responsibility for learning.

Students also have different preferred learning styles. Some are social learners, others prefer to study independently, others like a mix. Some learners are not happy working with a computer, either because of preferred learning style or lack of computer literacy. Some students may be competent at word processing but not at using the Internet, or vice versa. It may be necessary to implement special programs to assist learners in computer literacy or in developing appropriate approaches to technology-based learning. It may be necessary to provide a choice of delivery modes (face-to-face or distributed learning), but this will be an expensive option. Generally, though, the responsibility for dealing with different learning styles and preferences is likely to fall on the regular instructor, and well-conducted research should be able to provide guidance on the role of technology in meeting different preferred learning styles.

The need to adapt to the different needs of different learners is not really something unique that arises from the use of technology; technology merely exacerbates a general and already-existing problem. Nevertheless, carefully designed evaluation studies can provide invaluable feedback for teachers and decision makers about the appropriate role and impact of technology on an increasingly diverse student population. Teaching at universities and colleges will become more like fine-tuning a high performance engine.

Academic Technology Organization and Management

Although this book provides some strong guidelines (probably too strong) for the organization and management of technology for teaching and learning, there is still not enough experience to be confident that these will work, at least in all contexts. Experimentation and constant monitoring of organizational and management strategies, and particularly sharing of experience between different institutions, will be needed for some time. There is a need for some national, or better still, international benchmarking exercises to identify and measure best practice in the organization and management of technology for teaching purposes.

Cost-Benefit Analysis

Cost-benefit analysis attempts not only to relate the costs of activities to the benefits (and disadvantages) of a particular strategy but also to identify the underlying relationships between costs and benefits.

Two major cost-benefit studies of the use of new technologies have been developed in parallel in the United States and Canada. Jewett (1998) and Young (1998) have recently completed a study on behalf of the U.S. Department of Education. This study looked at twelve case studies using new technologies, which focused primarily on live instructional television and computer-based learning. The Canadian study (Bates and Bartolic, 1999), funded through the Canadian government's National Centers of Excellence-Telelearning project, focused on six case studies of on-line courses.

Although the U.S. and Canadian projects were separate, there has been close communication between the researchers in the two studies. Both projects developed somewhat similar methodologies for analyzing costs. The Canadian study collected three kinds of cost data—production and delivery costs, capital and recurrent costs, and fixed and variable costs—and identified three main areas of benefits—*performance-driven* benefits, including learning outcomes, student satisfaction, instructor satisfaction, and return on investment; *value-driven* benefits, including access, flexibility, and ease of use; and *value-added* benefits, such as reduced traffic and parking needs, spin-offs of new products and services, and increased revenue generation.

In each case study, data were collected under each of these categories (it should be noted that "benefits" could be negatively as well as positively assessed, for example, reducing instead of increasing access). Some of the preliminary findings from the Canadian studies (Bartolic and Bates, 1999) are as follows:

- *The cost structures of on-line learning are different from those of face-to-face teaching and print-based distance learning technologies.* Initial direct investment costs for on-line learning are higher than those for face-to-face teaching but lower than for print-based distance teaching; on-line learning costs have some economies of scale compared with face-to-face teaching, but the economies of scale for on-line learning are lower than those for print-based teaching because of the increased interaction between teachers and learners in on-line learning.
- *Start-up costs for specially designed on-line learning courses are substantial and often unanticipated,* especially in instructor time and administration. However, costs settle down quickly after the first offering of a course.
- *On-line learning courses can provide both quality learning and a return on investment,* even with unanticipated start-up costs.
- *Student reactions were mixed.* Reactions to on-line learning seem to be influenced by a number of factors. It seems to be more acceptable to students who cannot access the campus and to part-time students. There are definite trade-offs, not just in convenience and access but also in quality of learning. Many (and especially those working in a second language) preferred the asynchronous forms of on-line discussion and the international perspective such courses provided; others, especially the on-campus students, missed the spontaneity and simplicity of synchronous spoken communication
- *Design issues are just as critical for on-line learning as for other forms of teaching.* The organization and size of discussion forums are critical factors for success, as are the intervention strategies of tutors.
- *In the context in which the studies were done, the direct costs per student of specially designed on-line courses were similar to those of face-to-face instruction in the range of twenty to forty students per course per year over a four-year period.* Below twenty students per course, face-to-face teaching was cheaper per student; above forty students per course per year, on-line learning became increasingly cheaper per student. (These comparisons assumed similar student-teacher ratios for

both face-to-face and on-line teaching, and the effect of dropping below ten students per course was not measured.)

• *On-line learning allows for the development of courses that can be delivered on a global scale in a cost-effective manner.* But global courses are likely to represent a niche market, and demanding conditions need to be met to be successful.

• *In certain contexts, university-level on-line courses or programs can fully recover all their costs or make profits from student fees and franchises without government subsidies.*

• *Indirect (or value-added) as well as direct benefits of on-line learning were identified.* Indirect benefits include impact on campus transportation patterns, and hence on environmental issues, on classroom and other building requirements, and on the development of new products, services, and sources of revenue generation. The indirect benefits appear to be even more important than the direct benefits, although further research is needed in this area.

• *Indirect as well as direct costs of on-line learning were identified.* Indirect costs include network infrastructure and technical support services, use of central services such as registration and the finance office, buildings, and space requirements. Although on-line courses share some features with face-to-face teaching when it comes to indirect costs, there are significant areas where the indirect costs of on-line learning are different from those of face-to-face teaching, especially space and building requirements. Indirect as well as direct costs need to be considered when comparing face-to-face teaching with technology based teaching. More research is needed in this area.

It should be emphasized that these are preliminary results specific to certain contexts, and such studies need to be replicated in many other different contexts.

Conclusions

Because of the emerging context of technology-based teaching, especially for traditional campus-based universities and colleges, research and evaluation is essential. However, it is important to focus on the unique educational characteristics of these new technologies and to ensure that the wide range of factors influencing the successful use of new technologies is studied.

There is a need for constant evaluation and research of new technologies. In particular, the assessment of the educational and academic implications of their introduction and the potential indirect benefits of using new technologies suggests that research and evaluation should be a significant function of a central academic technology unit. This would help ensure that research and evaluation are focused on the needs of the institution and that the results and implications have wide impact throughout the institution.

Chapter Ten

Avoiding the Faustian Contract and Meeting the Technology Challenge

By this time, you may well have asked the question: Is it worth it? I must confess that I get tired merely thinking about what needs to be done. The implementation of the strategies so far outlined will present a major challenge to any university or college administration. Are they all necessary? Do the changes have to be as drastic as suggested? Could one not just let technology-based teaching gradually develop from the bottom up, and then deal with issues as they arise?

The Limitations of Planning

Most successful strategies are not totally planned in advance; as Mintzberg (1994) argues, they tend to emerge from patterns of small, individual decisions that can emanate from anywhere in an organization. I have been cautious about a traditional top-down strategic planning approach, putting more emphasis on developing vision and broad goals at a departmental level.

The significant feature of emergent strategy is that it is based on what has been *learned* from the pattern of the individual actions. So the planning and management process is an iterative one: strategies that emerge are learned, then applied in a deliberate and controlled way, and then modified as other, different strategies emerge. The strategies presented in this book are based on what has been learned from the result of many individual actions in a number of different institutions that are implementing technology-based teaching and learning.

In other words, this book is a little like a photograph, a moment captured in time. All the strategies recommended here should be seen in that light. They will need to change both in space and time; they will need to be adapted to local contexts and modified as further experience develops in using new technologies for teaching. Indeed, probably many other strategies are also necessary if technology is to be used successfully for teaching and learning.

Furthermore, timing is critical. There is a stage, for instance, where an institution needs to move from using "weak" criteria for funding that encourage maximum involvement of faculty members in developing new technology-based learning to using "strong" criteria for funding that will result in projects that are likely to succeed or be sustainable.

Then there is the cost of change. It takes time to design effective learning materials, to put technology systems in place. At the same time, the flow of conventional students and the necessity to conduct research does not stop. Thus, there is always a period where old and new systems are running in parallel. It may be several years after a project has started before the cost of developing it can be justified by improved learning outcomes or increased access.

The strategies proposed in this book are also all interrelated. There is no point in making major investments in technological infrastructure without a parallel development of a vision of how the institution wishes to teach over the next ten years. A "build it and they will come" approach without academic strategies for using the technology is a very expensive policy.

Another problem is caused by the impatience of senior managers or government. I know of several instances where someone has been called in and told to get a multimedia production department in a college up and running and fully cost-recoverable within two years. This is frankly impossible. It took more than a hundred years from the invention of the steam engine to Henry Ford's first production line. We are no more than twenty years into the so-called information revolution. Such revolutionary changes have to progress at a rate that can be absorbed by human beings, and in the case of higher education this means being absorbed by faculty, administrators, and students. The changes suggested in this book will need to be implemented over a period more like ten years than one or two years.

Nevertheless, the imperfect nature of planning and management does not diminish the need for deliberate strategies to implement effective technology-based teaching. Organizations such as universities and colleges tend to be conservative by nature. Without deliberate and coordinated actions, they are not so much unwilling as unable to adapt to the requirements for the successful use of technology for teaching.

When resources are limited or even diminishing, priorities have to be set. Funding reallocation will be essential to support technology-based teaching and learning.

A healthy organization learns from experience. That experience does not have to be confined to what happens in its own organizational boundary, but it can be learned through comparing best practice in other organizations and adapting it to the local context. The key here is flexibility and the willingness to learn from experience, both from inside and from outside the institution.

Resistance Is Futile?

There is also the option of not going down this road. An institution may decide to limit the use of technology for teaching to very specific purposes, such as teaching computer-aided design, where computers are absolutely essential. Technology may be used solely as a supplement to face-to-face teaching. Some institutions may decide to focus entirely on face-to-face teaching. I predict that there will be increasing differentiation between institutions, even institutions in the same sector, based on their use of technology for teaching and learning.

However, all alternative approaches that play down the role of technology in teaching contain high risk as well. More and more, learners will have developed extensive experience and skills in using information technologies in their nonacademic lives, and they will be increasingly unforgiving of institutions that seem out of touch with developments in the "real" world. Learners are likely to reject higher education institutions that do not integrate technology into the curriculum because of the perceived negative impact on their employability after graduation if they are not exposed to the use of technology. Furthermore, merely using technology as a supplement to traditional classroom teaching will increase costs without easily measurable or discernible benefits. An institution that deliberately shuns technology and places great emphasis on small group teaching, with a low student-teacher ratio, is likely to be a very expensive and hence highly exclusive institution.

What Do We Lose?

The increasing intrusion of technology into teaching forces the following questions to be addressed:

- What are the unique features of face-to-face teaching, and for what kinds of learner are these essential?
- What are the unique benefits of being on campus, and what kinds of learner will benefit most from this?
- What do the necessary processes of planning and managing technology do to the culture of an academic institution?

For a conventional campus-based institution, probably the most difficult challenge will be to achieve an appropriate balance between face-to-face and technology-based teaching and learning for the different kinds of students it will be serving. Distributed learning—as distinct from "pure" distance education—allows for a mix of campus-based and technology-based activities. There are potentially significant economic advantages from the use of distributed learning, particularly if it reduces the need for lectures and other forms of face-to-face teaching and thus reduces the need for attendance on campus.

What are the particular benefits of being on campus that cannot be (or are poorly) substituted by technology-based learning, and who will benefit most from this? For instance, electronic access to library facilities, especially over the Web, will increasingly allow just as wide a choice of readings as physical attendance at the campus library. Students can communicate flexibly and extensively with one another and their instructors through on-line discussion forums. Virtual labs can enable more intensive student interaction and a wider range of experiments than wet labs. Brilliant, moti-vating lectures that capture and synthesize the essence of a subject can be digitized on a CD-ROM.

So what in the way of teaching and learning cannot be done through technology? The list gets shorter each year. Nevertheless, there will always be some aspects of teaching and learning for which face-to-face teaching will be much more appropriate. However, no longer can it be taken as a general assumption that face-to-face teaching is always better. On the contrary, it will become increas-ingly important to justify it. The basis of the justification will in-creasingly move away from the nature of the subject matter and the teaching methodology to meeting the needs of particular learners for whom personal contact with teachers is important.

The fact is that many young people (and a few older ones) do not go to university or college just for academic learning purposes. They come for the social and cultural context. But how many in-stitutions really provide social and cultural events these days in an accessible and acceptable format for students? It seems to be a common complaint among faculty members that students are more "instrumental" and less interested in cultural and social ac-tivities on campus than in the past. This is no doubt because of their increasing need to work while studying, the large lecture classes, and the lack of availability of cultural functions supported by the institution as budgets come under increasing pressure. How-ever, if technology is to be a major means of delivering teaching, then it becomes even more vital to identify and provide social and cultural activities for those students who do need and want them.

At the same time, the changing demographics of higher edu-cation, with older students, returning graduates, and professionals needing updating, means that many learners do not need or care for these cultural activities to be provided as part of their studies. They do not feel the need to attend the campus, or cannot, even if they wanted to. The appropriate balance between technology-based teaching and face-to-face or campus-based teaching then will differ according to the needs of different types of learners. Never-theless, technology merely heightens the importance of defining exactly what the social and cultural roles of a campus-based uni-versity and college are, relating these to the differing needs of dif-ferent types of students and ensuring that these needs are met.

Perhaps the least obvious but potentially most important consequence of introducing technology is the change it will bring to the way faculty members do their work. The reduction in face-to-face contact with students will be negative for many faculty members (and positive for some). But more significant will be the impact on the independence and autonomy of faculty members. There will be a greater need for teamwork, planning, and training, and at least in the short term the use of technology is likely to require that much more time be spent and attention paid to teaching-related activities than has been the custom, at least in research universities. At the same time, we are finding that the challenge of teaching with new technologies has led to a revitalization of many professors' teaching.

Last, the planning and management strategies necessary for the successful implementation of new technologies really require a change in the culture of many institutions. A laissez-faire approach to teaching and the use of technology becomes increasingly difficult or expensive as the application of technology to teaching spreads throughout an institution. The danger is that planning and rationalizing the use of scarce resources may lead to top-down management and unacceptable restrictions on academic freedom. One of the most difficult challenges will be to build a postindustrial form of organization, with teaching and administration devolved to small and flexible units in an overall planning and management framework.

Can It Be Done?

It could be argued that the strategies proposed in this book require such fundamental changes in a university or college that the whole enterprise is unsustainable; it may be "better" to create new institutions from scratch.

I believe that this view underestimates the ability of some of the most intelligent and well-educated people in the world to learn, change, and take control of their own destinies. It also underestimates the pressure that is likely to be exerted on universities and colleges to change, by governments, by competition, and from within. Last, I ask skeptical professors: "Who is having the most fun in teaching: those struggling to serve increasingly large classes in the conventional system, or those who have embraced technology as a possible solution to increasing demands and reduced resources?"

So I predict that a number of universities and colleges will not be able to make the necessary changes and adaptation. However, others will protect their core activities by improving the quality of learning and the institution's cost-effectiveness, and they will do this through the intelligent use of technology. I hope this book helps those who decide to take this road.

References

American Productivity & Quality Center. *Today's Teaching and Learning: Leveraging Technology: Best Practice Report.* Houston: American Productivity & Quality Center, 1999.

Australian Graduate School of Management. *Managing the Introduction of Technology in the Delivery and Administration of Higher Education.* Canberra, Australia: Department of Employment, Education, Training, and Youth Affairs, 1996.

Bartolic, S., and Bates, A. W. "Investing in Online Learning: Potential Benefits and Limitations." *Canadian Journal of Communication,* 1999, *24*(3).

Bates, A. W. *Technology, Open Learning, and Distance Education.* New York: Routledge, 1995.

Bates, A. W., and Bartolic, S. *Assessing the Costs and Benefits of Telelearning: Six Case Studies.* Vancouver: University of British Columbia/National Centre of Excellence in Telelearning, 1999.

Bates, A. W., and Escamilla, J. "Crossing Boundaries: Making Global Distance Education a Reality." *Journal of Distance Education,* 1997, *12*(1, 2), 49–66.

Boyer, E. *Scholarship Reconsidered: Priorities for the Professoriate.* Princeton, N.J.: Carnegie Foundation for the Advancement of Teaching, 1990.

British Columbia Labour Force Development Board. *Training for What?* Victoria: Ministry of Skills, Training, and Labour, 1995.

Campion, M. "The Supposed Demise of Bureaucracy: Implication for Distance Education and Open Learning—More on the Post-Fordism Debate." *Distance Education,* 1995, *16*(2), 192–215.

Campion, M., and Renner, W. "The Supposed Demise of Fordism—Implications for Distance Education and Open Learning." *Distance Education,* 1992, *13*(1), 7–28.

Canadian Labour Market Productivity Centre. "The Linkages Between Education and Training and Canada's Economic Performance." *Quarterly Labour Market and Productivity Review,* Winter 1989.

Clark, R. "Reconsidering Research on Learning from Media." *Review of Educational Research,* 1983, *53*(4), 445–460.

Conference Board of Canada. *Employability Skill Profile: The Critical Skills Required of the Canadian Workforce.* Ottawa, Ontario: Conference Board of Canada, 1991.

Conway, K. "Designing Classrooms for the 21st Century." In D. Oblinger and S. Rush (eds.), *The Future Compatible Classroom.* Bolton, MA: Anker, 1998.

Daniel, J. *Mega-Universities and Knowledge Media: Technology Strategies for Higher Education.* London: Kogan Page, 1998.

Dearing, R. *Higher Education in the Learning Society: Report of the National Committee.* London: Her Majesty's Stationery Office–National Committee of Inquiry into Higher Education, 1997.

Dolence, M., and Norris, D. *Transforming Higher Education: A Vision for Learning in the 21st Century.* Ann Arbor, MI: Society for College and University Planning, 1995.

Drouin, M.-J. *Workforce Literacy: An Economic Challenge for Canada.* Montréal: Hudson Institute, 1990.

Farnes, N. "Modes of Production: Fordism and Distance Education." *Open Learning,* 1993, *8*(1), 10–20.

Feenberg, A. "Distance Learning: Promise or Threat?" *National Crosstalk,* 1999, *7*(1), 12–14.

Finnegan, D. "Transforming Faculty Roles." In M. Peterson, D. Dill, L. A. Mets, and Associates, *Planning and Management for a Changing Environment.* San Francisco: Jossey-Bass, 1997, pp. 479–501.

Fritz, R. *The Path of Least Resistance.* New York: Columbine, 1989.

Graves, W., Henshaw, R., Oberlin, J., and Parker, A. "Infusing Information Technology into the Academic Process." In M. Peterson, D. Dill, L. Mets, and Associates, *Planning and Management for a Changing Environment.* San Francisco: Jossey-Bass, 1997, pp. 432–452.

Green, F. "Survey of Information Technology Planning." *Campus Computing,* 1998.

Holt, D., and Thompson, D. "Responding to the Technological Imperative: The Experience of an Open and Distance Education Institution." *Distance Education,* 1995, *16*(1), 43–64.

Holt, D., and Thompson, D. "Managing Information Technology in Open and Distance Higher Education." *Distance Education,* 1998, *19*(2), 197–227.

Institute for Higher Education Policy. *The Tuition Puzzle.* Washington, D.C.: Institute for Higher Education Policy, 1999.

Jewett, F. *BRIDGE: A Simulation Model for Comparing the Costs of Expanding a Campus using Distributed Instruction versus Classroom Instruction.* Seal Beach: Chancellor's Office, California State University, 1998.

Katz, R., and Associates. *Dancing with the Devil: Information Technology and the New Competition in Higher Education.* San Francisco: Jossey-Bass, 1999.

Kunin, R. "Fewer Full-Time Jobs." *Canadian Business Review.* 1988, *15*(2), 26–27.

Laurillard, D. *Rethinking University Teaching.* London: Routledge, 1995.

Le Grew, D. "Global Knowledge: Superhighway or Super Gridlock?" In *Applications of Media and Technology in Higher Education.* Chiba, Japan: National Institute of Multimedia Education, 1995.

Marchese, T. "Not-So-Distant Competitors: How New Providers are Remaking the Postsecondary Marketplace." *American Association of Higher Education Bulletin,* May 1998.

Mason, R. *Globalising Education.* London: Routledge, 1998.

Mintzberg, H. *The Rise and Fall of Strategic Planning.* New York: Free Press, 1994.

Moore, M., and Thompson, M. *The Effects of Distance Education: A Summary of the Literature.* University Park: American Center for Distance Education, Pennsylvania State University, 1990.

Moran, C. "Strategic Information Technology Planning in Higher Education." In D. Oblinger and S. Rush (eds.), *The Future Compatible Campus.* Bolton, MA: Anker, 1998, pp. 151–163.

Noble, D. "Digital Diploma Mills: The Automation of Higher Education." [http://www.journet.com/twu/deplomamills.html] 1997.

Noble, D. "Digital Diploma Mills, Part 2: The Coming Battle Over Online Instruction." [http://www.chass.utoronto.ca/~buschert/noble] 1998.

Noblitt, J. "Making Ends Meet: A Faculty Perspective on Computing and Scholarship." In D. Oblinger and S. Rush (eds.), *The Future Compatible Campus.* Bolton, MA: Anker, 1998.

Open Learning Agency. *Lifelong Learning and Human Resource Development.* Burnaby, B.C.: Open Learning Agency, 1992.

Peters, O. "Distance Teaching and Industrial Production." In D. Sewart, D. Keegan, and B. Holmberg (eds.), *Distance Education: International Perspectives.* London: Croom Helm, 1983.

Porter, M. *Canada at the Crossroads: The Reality of a New Competitive Environment.* Ottawa: Business Council on National Issues-Government of Canada, 1991.

Postman, N. *Technopoly: The Surrender of Culture to Technology.* New York: Vintage Books, 1992.

Reich, R. "The Real Economy." *Atlantic Monthly,* Feb. 1991.

Renner, W. "Post-Fordist Visions and Technological Solutions: Educational

Technology and the Labour Process." *Distance Education,* 1995, *16*(2), 284–330.

Resmer, M., Mingle, J. and Oblinger, D. *Computers for All Students: A Strategy for Universal Access to Information Resources.* Denver: State Higher Education Executive Officers, 1995.

Ross, D. "Project Management in the Development of Instructional Material for Distance Education: An Australian Overview." *American Journal of Distance Education,* 1991, *5*(2), 24–30.

Rowley, D., Lujan, H., and Dolence, M. *Strategic Choices for the Academy.* San Francisco: Jossey-Bass, 1998.

Rumble, G. "Labour Market Theories and Distance Education: Industrialization and Distance Education." *Open Learning,* 1995, *10*(1), 10–20.

Rumble, G. *The Costs and Economics of Open and Distance Learning.* London: Kogan Page, 1997.

Russell, T. *The No Significant Difference Phenomenon.* Raleigh: North Carolina State University Office of Instructional Telecommunications, 1999.

Schramm, W. *Big Media, Little Media.* Thousand Oaks, Calif.: Sage, 1974.

Senge, P. *The Fifth Discipline.* New York: Doubleday, 1990.

Smith, S. *Report: Commission of Inquiry on Canadian University Education.* Ottawa: Association of Universities and Colleges of Canada, 1991.

Statistics Canada. *Internet Use by Households: Household Internet Use Survey.* Ottawa: Statistics Canada, 1998.

Statistics Canada. *The Daily,* Apr. 23, 1999.

Weimer, B. "Assumptions About University-Industry Relationships in Continuing Professional Education: A Reassessment." *European Journal of Education,* 1992, *27*(4).

Wilson, A. W., and Cervero, R. M. "The Song Remains the Same: The Selective Tradition of Technical Rationality in Adult Education Program Planning Theory." *International Journal of Lifelong Education,* 1997, *16*(2), 84–108.

Young, F. *Case Studies in Evaluating the Benefits and Cost of Mediated Instruction and Distributed Learning: Synopses/Summaries of Eight Cases.* Seal Beach: Chancellor's Office, California State University, 1998.

Index